Algrove Publishing Limited
1090 Morrison Drive
Ottawa, Ontario
Canada K2H 1C2

Canadian Cataloguing in Publication Data

Hodgson, Fred. T. (Frederick Thomas), 1836-1919
    Hodgson's Art of wood carving

(Classic reprint series)
Originally published under title: Easy lessons in the art of practical
    wood carving. Chicago : F.J. Drake, 1905.
Includes index.
ISBN 1-894572-10-6

    1. Wood-carving. I. Title. II. Title: Art of wood carving. III. Title: Easy lessons in the art of practical wood carving. IV. Series: Classic reprint series (Ottawa, Ont.)

NK9704.H7 2000   736'.4   C00-900968-X

Printed in Canada
#11000

PUBLISHER'S NOTE

F red Hodgson was one of the most prolific writers of his era.
Writing in a time when authors pretended to cover all knowledge
in a given field, Hodgson painted with a broad brush, covering an
amazing range of subjects in a most optimistic style. In doing so, he
was one of the earliest writers to encourage readers to try activities
with which they had no experience.

Leonard G. Lee, Publisher
Ottawa
September, 2000

SHEIK-EL-BELAD.
Ancient Egyptian Wood Carving. (Circa 4000 B.C.)

Easy Lessons in the Art of
Practical Wood Carving

SUITED TO THE WANTS OF CARPENTERS, JOINERS, AMATEURS AND PROFESSIONAL WOOD CARVERS

BEING A PRACTICAL MANUAL AND GUIDE TO ALL KINDS OF WOOD CARVING, INCLUDING CHIP CARVING, FLAT CARVING, INCISED WORK AND FIGURE CARVING, TOGETHER WITH AN ESSAY ON THE PRINCIPLES OF DESIGN FOR CARVED WORK OF ALL KINDS

By
FRED T. HODGSON, M.O.A.A.

AUTHOR OF

"Practical Treatise on the Use of the Steel Square," "Modern Carpentry," "Common-Sense Stair Building and Handrailing," "Drawing Self-Taught," "Hardwood Finisher," "Modern Estimator and Contractor's Guide," etc.

Over Two Hundred Illustrations, Diagrams and Designs

CHICAGO, U.S.A.
FREDERICK J. DRAKE & CO., PUBLISHERS
1905

TYPOGRAPHY BY
MARSH, AITKEN & CURTIS COMPANY, CHICAGO

PREFACE

The author and compiler of this work prepared a series of articles on Carving for "The National Builder" a few years ago, and also a series on the same subject for "The Carpenter," the official organ of "The Brotherhood of American Carpenters." Since these articles were prepared, the writer has received many requests asking that the articles be put in book form, and in compliance with these requests I have selected from these articles what I consider to be the better portions, have amended many of them, rewritten others, and added much new matter, for which I am indebted to "The Woodworker," "Wood Carving," by George Jack, "Wood Carving for Amateurs," by David Denning, also to several other standard works on wood carving, so that the reader of this book—although he may have read the articles referred to—will have an almost entirely new phase of the subject placed before him.

Besides culling the best from the articles referred to, and embodying it in the present work, I have selected from many sources such matter, instructions and illustrations as I thought would be suited to the wants of the American workman who aspires to become a carver of wood. The designs in the first portion of the work are purposely made simple and easy to work in order to lead the workman steadily on to greater efforts.

I have gone to some length in describing the tools required, the methods of using them, and the care they demand, giving such rules as long and successful experience has taught as the best. This portion of the work is, perhaps, the most important to the young student, for without a thorough knowledge of the tools and a complete mastery over them, no person can ever become a good wood carver; indeed, a complete control of all the tools necessary in this fascinating art is in itself an education of a high order.

The section on "Chip Carving," with the illustrations and designs given, is in a measure a complete treatise in itself, and may be reckoned as such by the amateur workman who does not care to follow up the art to a higher plane.

In a work of this kind our province is to keep as much as possible to things appertaining to architectural work. Carved woodwork, as an accessory to architecture, is an ornamental and refined detail that presents an infinite charm to the cultivated mind.

It is a mistake, and a serious one, to carve wood too fragile, or indeed fragile at all. There is no real skill, in point of fact, in too much undercutting. In figure work, too, uplifted and extended hands or arms, and especially pointing fingers, are a weakness and a snare. Much anxious labor is spent in their creation, and is simply thrown away, yea, and worse, for in a few short years, maybe only weeks or days, those projecting parts, obtruding from niche or newel, will surely be knocked off by some careless duster. Of course the broken pieces may be mended, stuck together with glue, but is there anything more humiliating to an ambitious craftsman than to see a statuette, the project of days or weeks, thus mutilated? Yet whose is the fault? Not altogether that of the careless one who does the actual damage. Surely a much larger amount of blame must belong to the unthinking and unmindful workman who, forgetful of everything but the fact that—in his own eyes—he is doing something wonderful upon his bench, makes that which cannot be expected to have a long life in the position for which it is destined.

A boy—a girl for that matter—cannot begin to learn the art of wood carving too early. Thirteen years old is a good age; fourteen quite late enough. It is a great mistake to keep a youngster at school until he begins to fancy he knows more than his father or any one else. We never knew any one who first went to the trade, say at eighteen or nineteen, turn out really well. A boy learning in a good shop (if an apt pupil) by the time he is of age feels competent to hold his own with any ordinary workman. That is one of the grandest and happiest feelings a young man can possess when starting the battle of life on his own account.

It is a curious but well-known practical fact that a youth who has served a time at wood carving (if he possesses ordinary application) can always learn to carve stone or marble afterwards, and with a few years' practice will be able to hold his own with any follower of either of the latter branches. On the other hand, we never knew a stone or marble carver who could carve wood properly. Some of them may think they can, but they really cannot do it. The knack of treating the grain in wood must always be acquired in youth, or it will never be thoroughly mastered later on. The stone or marble carver who tries his hand at wood tears rather than cuts the stuff, and when he finds he cannot do it properly, swears, and there's an end of it! Some of the most successful

PREFACE

artists who ever lived commenced their brilliant careers as wood carvers.

The good carpenter finds no trouble whatever in making simple carvings, because of his knowledge of cutting and manipulating woodwork in a hundred forms. His thorough knowledge of the use of tools is half the trade itself, and the step from good joinery or cabinet making to carving is comparatively an easy one, and we may say right here that this book is prepared more especially for the carpenter, joiner, and cabinetmaker who know something of woodworking than for those who intend to follow wood carving alone as a profession, though the work contains much that will interest and instruct the professional, particularly in the matter of designs and illustrations.

That the book has its faults and shortcomings goes without saying. What book has not? But it is thought to be as good as any other like book on the subject, and is much cheaper, and in a number of particulars is superior to other books of the kind. That it is more suited to the wants of the ordinary woodworker, the editor feels confident, knowing, as he does, just exactly what their wants are in this direction, and on this ground, along with its other good qualities, the book is placed in the hands of its readers with an assurance that it will be welcomed by thousands who have read the writer's other works.

FRED T. HODGSON.

COLLINGWOOD, ONTARIO, April 1st, 1905.

Practical Wood Carving

INTRODUCTORY

Harry Hems, the celebrated English carver, says: "No doubt, as a matter of position it is better to be a good wood carver than a good joiner, but a poor carver is a long way down the scale below the handy carpenter. It is not every one that has the natural 'gift' to become a really clever carver of wood. Parents should ever be careful to give their sons several months' probation ere the fate of the youngster is decided upon. If a boy has no real talent for wood carving he never ought to be apprenticed to the profession, for hard work and the most diligent application will rarely make up for lack of natural ability. Of all the many hundred businesses that go strictly hand in hand with the building trade, that of a figure carver in wood for architectural purposes has its fewest representatives. It is probable that in all England at the present moment there are not forty men who can carve even decent figures in wood. The position, therefore, of these skilled craftsmen is an envied one; there is a constant demand for their services; they command good money, and their occupation, always varied and never representing really hard manual labor, is one of the most delightful pursuits a man can possibly follow.

"Ordinary wood carvers do not pretend to be masters of the figure, and when at rare intervals they attempt it the results are seldom successful. A great gulf exists between figure and foliage work. For whilst the foliage carver is quite lost upon the human form divine when he attempts to produce it in wood, so the figure carver is almost equally at sea when he turns his hand to ornament. If he tries it, and he generally does so hesitatingly, he is rarely successful.''

He also gives some excellent advice to beginners, which is deemed worthy of being quoted at this point. "Always stand to your work, and don't lean over it too much. Too much leaning over tends to laziness. I have seen small seats in the top of a spiked stick. The latter steadies itself on the floor, and the carver will sit thereon, work, and swing his body round with it as occasion requires. But it has not a good look about it, and does not stamp a diligent and smart man.''

"Although it is a good rule always to do work in the solid, it often happens that pateræ, etc., are put into hollows after the latter are run through. The best way to carve them, under these circumstances, is to have a hollow made the same size in pine, and glue each individual rosette therein with paper between the pine and the material carved. After the latter is finished it can be lifted out by a chisel as easily as shelling peas, as the paper splits at the slightest purchase of the tool. It is, however, always a matter of intense regret to me to see rosettes stuck on. Everything should be cut out of the solid wood. It is this wholesome practice that makes our average work so much better than the best produced in Belgium and Germany. In the latter two countries, it seems to me, nothing is in the solid that can be glued on.''

These hints and suggestions given out by a veteran

carver are worthy of the serious consideration of every person who intends to try his or her hand at the art.

Carving is an art in which various advantages are combined, for not only is this art beautiful and excellent in itself, but it may further be regarded in the light of a stepping stone to greater things. In proof of this we need only glance at the history of some of the most famous painters and sculptors, many of whom, we read, rose to greatness from the practice of the comparatively humble art of wood carving.

It is an employment which can be taken up at any time, and can be as easily relinquished; for the carver's fingers, when once facility has been learnt, do not easily lose their cunning from disuse. Although considerable practice, combined with natural aptitude, is necessary to enable any one to become a really skilled carver, the time spent in cultivating this talent will be by no means wasted, even should nothing beyond the merest mediocrity be attained.

A very slight amount of practice will enable any ordinarily skillful person to do simple carving, which, for the encouragement of beginners, it may be said, is often as pleasing as more pretentious efforts, especially when these are not accompanied by great manual dexterity.

On the score of small cost much might be urged in favor of wood carving as a recreative art, but, beyond calling attention to the fact that a large outlay is not necessary at the commencement, little need be said here. A few dollars will procure all the tools that are really requisite for a beginning, and as the carver will, if he be wise, only get others as he requires them, the additional expenditure is hardly felt.

When discussing the necessary "plant," which

includes the tools, materials, and everything which is required in setting up the workshop, various little makeshifts and expedients by which much may be contrived without any serious outlay will be suggested.

Wood carving, which at first sight may seem to resemble in some degrees the more mechanical employment of carpentry, nevertheless differs from it in this important particular that, unlike purely manual pursuits which can be mastered by any one possessing a fair amount of intelligence and mechanical skill, it demands in addition to these qualities a certain "feeling," or in other words, talent; this "feeling," or whatever we may choose to call it, it is obviously impossible to teach; the germ must at least to some degree be innate in the artist; much, however, may be done in the way of fostering and encouraging it.

Although a knowledge of carpentry, as before stated, will be an aid to the wood carver, it is not essential. The skill in this line need be but rudimentary, though the greater the acquaintance with it so much the easier will it be to become an adept in carving work of all kinds.

But it must be understood that a person may be highly skilled in carpentry without having a particle of the taste or talent requisite for artistic carving. However great the natural talent may be, it is three parts wasted if it be fettered by clumsy fingers, and therefore those who suffer from this defect should make every effort to overcome and correct it. It is also well to acquire a knowledge of the different woods employed, their nature and various qualities, and the purposes to which they are best adapted. Also it would be advisable to learn the names and purposes of the common tools in use amongst carpenters, together with the ordinary technical terms, such as dovetailing, mortising, rabbeting, and such like. By these means the carver will be enabled to give clear and intelligible directions in regard to the materials, etc., which will be required in the course of the work.

While on this subject it may be as well to say here once for all that it is not the intention in the following pages to explain the names and use of tools which do not specially pertain to the carver's art. Those which are used by other workers in wood may be and undoubtedly are useful to the carver, especially if, as many amateurs do, he wishes to "make up" his own work. If he cannot do so there is rarely any difficulty in getting what is required done by a cabinet-maker, who is to be preferred to a joiner or carpenter, as he is more accustomed to small work. As many ladies now take up carving as an amusement, this book will at any rate commend itself to them.

Although it is impossible to acquire skill, or what has been previously referred to as "feeling," from this or any other treatise on carving, the beginner will be helped over the initial difficulties, or perhaps it should rather be said started on the right way. If the directions are carefully attended to and put in practice there is little doubt that a fair measure of success will be attained. Great skill and power to execute important work cannot be derived from books, or indeed from tuition of any kind. They must depend almost entirely on the workman's ability and application.

For any work, of course, the first requisites are the tools, and these I will endeavor to describe in the following and subsequent chapters, as certain styles of carving require different kinds of tools from other styles of carving.   However, there are some tools which are common to all kinds of work and it is these I will deal with first, and take in the others as they are required for the work under discussion.

In the last chapter of this work it is my intention not only to deal with carvings alone, but to show a number of examples of useful carved work put together, and give instructions for putting it together. This, while not perhaps of much use to the expert joiner or cabinetmaker, will prove useful to the amateur and the new beginner.

I have thought that these few preliminary remarks might be necessary so that the text following may not be padded with the explanations already given.

CHAPTER I

CARVERS' TOOLS AND APPLIANCES

We will suppose that the student is anxious to make a practical commencement in his studies. The first consideration will be to procure a set of tools, and we propose in this place to describe those which will answer the purpose of a beginner, as well as to look generally at others in common use among craftsmen.

The tools used by carvers consist for the most part of chisels and gouges of different shapes and sizes. The number of tools required by professional carvers for one piece of work varies in proportion to the elaborateness of the carving to be done. They may use from half a dozen on simple work up to twenty or thirty for the more intricate carvings, this number being a selection out of a larger stock reaching perhaps as many as a hundred or more. Many of these tools vary only in size and sweep of cutting edge. Thus, chisels and gouges are to be had ranging from $\frac{1}{16}$ of an inch to 1 inch wide, with curves or "sweeps" in each size graduated between a semicircle to a curve almost flat. Few carvers, however, possess such a complete stock of tools as would be represented by one of each size and shape manufactured; such a thing is not required; an average number of, say, seventy tools, will always give sufficient variety of size and sweep for general purposes; few pieces of work will require the use of more than half of these in its execution.

The beginner, however, need not possess more than

17

from twelve to twenty-four, and may even make a start with fewer. It is a good plan to learn the uses of a few tools before acquiring a complete set, as by this means, when difficulties are felt in the execution of work, a tool of known description is sought for and purchased with a foreknowledge of its advantages.

This is the surest way to gain a distinct knowledge of the varieties of each kind of tool and their application to the different purposes of design.

It is not at all uncommon for those who have not devoted any attention to practical carving to imagine that the work is done with "some kind of a knife." Let the beginner at once dismiss this notion from his mind, for with the exception of a special one for chip carving, to which a chapter is devoted, a knife is not used.

The ordinary cutting tools are chisels and gouges of many shapes and sizes. A complete set of them is not in the least necessary for a beginner.

The various carving tools most needful, though few in number, must be selected with great care and judgment, the quality far outweighing the quantity; indeed, a few, let us say twelve or eighteen, really good tools, well cared for, and with which you are thoroughly acquainted, will produce good work at first.

They are to be bought in "sets," but as these are specially prepared for amateurs they cannot be indiscriminately recommended. Some of them are good, but many are such as no experienced carver could use with satisfactory results. These words of caution are deemed necessary, as it is by no means uncommon for the amateur sets to be much more pleasing in appearance than the more workmanlike tools. These, in comparison, are often rough looking, but the quality is generally better, and the original cost little, if any, greater. Good carving tools are to be had from any respectable tool dealer, if a fair price is paid for them, and, as a guide to price, tool dealers' catalogues may be consulted with advantage.

As before stated, two dozen tools are as many as are required on first setting up; though a dozen would be a far better number to begin with, as much work can be done with them, and others can be added as required.

It is difficult to say with certainty what the selection should be, but as the most useful tools for ordinary work are flat gouges, four of them, ⅛, ¼, ⅜ and ½ inch sizes, will be a fair proportion.

These tools are almost flat like chisels, but instead of being quite so, have a slight curve. Between the flat gouge and that with the "quickest" curve there are several with varying degrees of sweep, and two of a medium quickness may be added in, say ⅜ inch size, as well as one of the "quickest."

These latter, when of the smallest size, are known as veiners, from their frequent use in carving the veins or small grooves in leaves. Till some measure of facility has been gained with larger tools their employment will be found difficult.

Chisels are of two kinds, those with the ends ground straight across and those with bevel ends. These latter are known as skew or corner chisels, and next to the flat gouges are perhaps the most useful tools of the carver. One of each kind of chisel in the smallest (¹⁄₁₆ inch) and ½ inch sizes will be useful, but in these, as indeed in other tools, the selection must chiefly depend on the style of carving the worker prefers.

A parting or, as it is commonly called, a V tool is

another useful one, and is almost indispensable, but at first it is difficult to use properly. The reason for its familiar designation will be recognized. The ¼ inch size will be most useful to the beginner.

All the tools that will be required at first are what are known as "straight." All varieties are, however, made in both "bent" and "curved." Their object is to allow of their edges cutting in places which could not be reached with the straight tools. The curved variety is of comparatively little use, as the beginner will find that almost everything he is likely to attempt can be done with straight or bent tools.

If any bent tool is got with the first lot of tools it should be a bent chisel of the smallest size, as it will sometimes be useful in cutting away the ground in places which could not well be reached by the other tools.

In choosing these tools do not be too easily satisfied, or inclined to think that the first that is seen will suit, but rather take time and examine each separately until those of the right sort are found; for, as in other matters, there are tools and tools. Choose, then, those that are long and slender, and of which the points when pressed on the table feel somewhat springy; they should also be slightly, almost imperceptibly, bent up towards the end; this curve must not be exaggerated, or it will weaken the tool.

Sets of tools for amateurs are generally sold handled, but for ordinary carvers' tools the handles are supplied separately. They can be fitted on by the tool dealer; if, however, the carver prefers to do this, great care must be taken to set them in very straight, as otherwise the tool will not work truly. The handle itself should be small but long, about one-half of the whole length; this is especially necessary in those tools with which a mallet is used, in order to have plenty of room for the hand to grasp it without fear of being hit. The length of handle for the smaller tools, which are chiefly used without the mallet, must be regulated by the size of the hand, the forefinger of which should rest on or a little below the hilt, while the butt end rests in and is pushed forward by the hollow of the palm. The form of ready-made handles is generally round, but an octagonal or hexagonal shape, with the thickest part in the middle rather than at the end, is a very useful variety, as it thus affords a firmer grasp for the fingers. Handles should be made of some hard wood, such as ebony, rosewood or box, or indeed any wood capable of being made very smooth and highly polished; if otherwise, the palm of the hand would be liable to be galled by the constant friction and pressure. This is a point of great importance, and should always be borne in mind, for the very best carver could hardly fail to turn out bad work when wincing under a blistered hand, and nothing is so certain to cause this as an ill-made or rough handle. For this reason it is well to avoid using a tool the handle for which has been beaten and frayed with blows from the mallet, without repolishing it with a file or sandpaper.

If, instead of the modest number of tools I have suggested, a greater quantity is purchased, it will be found very convenient to have the handles of various woods and colors, so that each may be known at a glance; thus, for instance, the smaller gouges might be of rosewood, the largest cherry wood, the chisel ebony, and others of boxwood; also it is convenient to have a number or any special mark branded on the handle to denote the size; by this means no time is wasted in searching for any particular implement, which would certainly be the case were they all alike, without any means of distinguishing them. All these little matters, trivial and hardly worth noticing though they may seem, are nevertheless, as long experience has taught, of very material assistance.

In any but the lightest work a mallet of some kind is necessary, for no tool should be pounded with a hammer. The carver's mallet should have a round head exactly like a stone mason's mallet, though an ordinary mallet will serve the purpose, but the former is preferable.

Wood carving may be said to be of three kinds, the simplest of which is *Surface Carving;* it might be called engraving, and is appropriate for the adornment of objects that are handled, such as caskets, book racks, book covers, glove and other small boxes. This work is better known as *Chip Carving,* of which I will have more to say later on. Surface carving is most effective when done on a polished (shellacked) surface, where a design, say of leaves and blossoms, is left bright, and the background is roughened or grained by stamping and afterward darkened by oiling. Another method of carving is called incised work. It is relief intaglio, the design being outlined and modeled, leaving the remaining surface of the wood untouched. This method is sometimes, though incorrectly, called intaglio carving. But intaglio cutting or engraving is the reverse of relief, such as a cameo; it is an engraving or carving which, when impressed on wax or plaster, gives a raised or relief design. Incised carving is modeled in relief, but done without lowering or cutting away the remaining surface. A more general and more artistic method of carving is relief work, where the design when completed appears wholly raised above the uniform depth. The background may be smoothly finished or it may be grained by stamping. The rough background, absorbing the oil, appears to give a heightened effect to the carving.

The tools shown in Fig. 1 are about all that will be required for a start. The shape of the tool is given, also the cut it gives. An expert workman may use a larger number of tools, but for the beginner the following list is amply sufficient; as he advances he can add others, as the work in hand may demand. The following eleven tools will serve for all kinds of carving except perhaps modeling in the round, yet they are used in this kind of carving in some cases. The first of the illustrations, the carver's chisels, are called by the trade firmers, to distinguish them from the chisel used by carpenters. Of these useful tools there are a great many

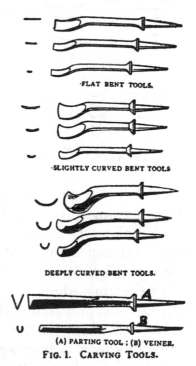

FLAT BENT TOOLS.

SLIGHTLY CURVED BENT TOOLS

DEEPLY CURVED BENT TOOLS.

(A) PARTING TOOL : (B) VEINER.
FIG. 1. CARVING TOOLS.

sizes, from $\frac{1}{32}$ of an inch to 2 inches in width. The smaller sizes are called picks; carvers generally make them themselves. Of chisels select two sizes or three, one $\frac{3}{16}$ of an inch and one ½ inch. The second lot are very useful tools for cutting into corners, veining and other purposes. Of the tools choose two sizes, one ¼ of an inch and one ½ inch.   Of the gouges shown, select one ¼ of an inch and one ⅝ of an inch.   Gouges are of all magnitudes of curves, from the slightest curve that might almost be taken for flat to the half of an oval.   Of these select one ⅛ and one ⅜ of an inch.

When the tools are purchased they are not ground, neither have they handles.   The tools must first be set in handles.   To put the handles on, the tool is held in a vise, the handle is pushed onto the tongue of the tool and twisted backward and forward to make the hole in the handle larger.   This should be continued until it can be pushed within three-quarters of an inch of the shoulder of the tool; it is then driven right home.   This method prevents the handle from splitting.   Buck Brothers of New England make very good carvers' tools, but probably the best that can be bought are made by Addis, but they are very high priced.

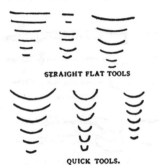

STRAIGHT FLAT TOOLS

QUICK TOOLS.

FIG. 2. CUTTING EDGES OF TOOLS.

The cutting edges of a variety of tools are shown in Fig. 2, most of which will be required by the workman as he advances in the art.

Fig. 3 shows a number of punch points which will come in for diapering or padding the background of the work

FIG 3. PUNCHES.

in many cases.   Most of these punches the workman will be able to make himself out of round and square bars of steel of the proper section.   The steel can be softened by heating and then let cool gradually, after which the pattern on the end may be worked out with a file, cold chisel or drill, as the pattern may demand; after which the steel must be heated to a cherry red color and then plunged into oil or into a stick of sealing wax. This process will make the tool quite hard enough for ordinary purposes.

A very useful punch, and one that is easily made, is shown in Fig. 4, also the impression it makes. This

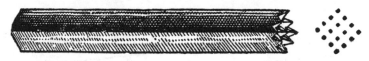

FIG. 4.

style of padding is very often used. It is quite effective.

Every carver should provide himself with a bench. He may make one for himself according to the size and construction shown in the illustration, Fig. 5. The top should be made of two 11 x 2 inch boards, and, as steadiness is the main feature to be aimed at, the joints should have some care. Those in illustration are shown to be formed by checking one piece of wood over the other, with shoulders to resist the lateral strain. Proper tenons would be better, but more difficult to make. It must have a projecting edge at the front and ends to receive the clamps. The bench should have a joiner's "bench-screw" attached to the back leg for holding work which is to be carved on its edges or ends. The feet should be secured to the floor by means of iron brackets, as considerable force is applied in carving hard wood, which may move the bench bodily unless it is secured or is very heavy. Professional carvers use a bench which is composed of beech planks three or four inches in thickness and of such a length as can be accommodated by the room available.

Another bench, somewhat more elaborate than that shown in Fig. 5, is shown in Fig. 6. This has a top 36 × 36 inches, which is 1½ inches in thickness; it is not necessary to be hard wood; red or white pine is quite strong and suitable enough; it should be square

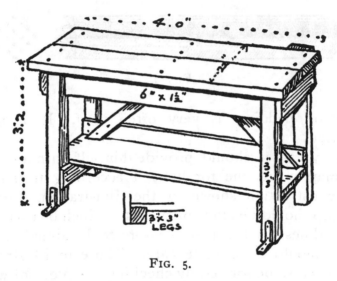

FIG. 5.

edged and should project 3 inches clear of the legs and rails. The legs and rails should be of fairly heavy material, as regards size, to give the whole bench sufficient weight. An open shelf and a drawer for the tools should be provided. The dimensions of the bench and its parts are given in the sketch. A bench like this has many advantages; it is strong and heavy, it enables the learner to get to both the end and side of his work, it provides accommodation for his tools, the work is easily fastened to it, and one of the greatest advantages is that there is room enough in the center for a light to be placed, whether electric, gas, or lamp light, without anything being able to obstruct its free passage to the student's work.

The bench shown in Fig. 7 is quite different from the previous ones, but is the one preferred by Harry Hems, and is from an illustration of his making.

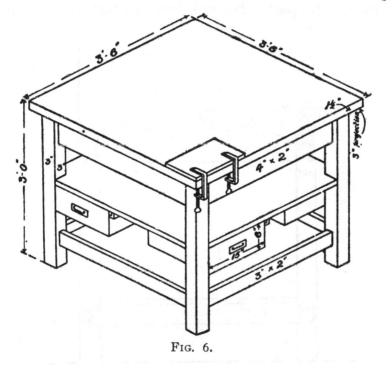

FIG. 6.

Regarding it he has the following to say, which I think worthy of production at this point:

"A wood carver dearly loves his bench, and is not altogether quite at home without it. In this he differs from the stone carver, who prefers to carve what he is about *in situ*. A carver's bench is quite different in construction from a joiner's; the latter is portable and may be put anywhere at will, the former is stationary and should always be fixed under a window.

"The carver's bench is also somewhat higher than a joiner's, *i.e.*, it must be 3 feet 2½ inches high. The main portion, that which is actually worked upon, should be of well-seasoned beech, 4 inches thick and 1 foot 8 inches wide, firmly planted upon framing of the same material, with upright supports (4 × 3 inches) about 3 feet apart. Behind this, *i.e.*, farthest from the

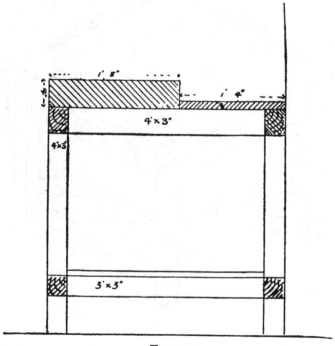

FIG. 7.

worker, it should be widened out by a deal plank 1 foot 4 inches wide or thereabouts, fixed so that its surface is 3 inches below the actual working bench. This allows the tools to be spread upon it without their handles projecting quite so high as the top of the bench itself. Thus a large job may always be turned about without in any way interfering with the tools which lie upon the lower level. The height given is an excellent and comfortable one for the average workman, whilst a short one or boy can always suit his own convenience, as necessary, by having a block or two to stand upon. About 1 foot from the ground there should be a shelf of 1¼ inch pine. This is always found most useful, not only to stow away odd pieces of stuff that are sure to come in handy some day, but also to put a foot upon now and again when a change of position is desired. In one of my own studios we have a continuous bench measuring 70 feet long. It offers fairly ample accommodation for twenty carvers, *i.e.*, allowing 3 feet 6 inches for each craftsman.

"As it is essential for light that a carver's bench be fixed under windows, it is also necessary that the latter be provided with blinds. The head is bent forward whilst its owner is at work, and in warm weather the sun pours upon it inconveniently.

"It is only careless wood carvers who work upon the actual bench itself. There should always be cutting boards of 1 inch yellow pine between the bench and the job in hand. These not only save the benches, but if work has to be pared or cut through, the softer material saves the under edges of the finished carvings from breaking away. The benches may be bored in a couple of places to take the hold-fast, and a couple of smaller holes at convenient distances be made for the bench-screw. For the latter, bored blocks are required to pack up the screw under the bench board, and care should be taken never to fasten down the hold-fast upon the work to be carved with hard wood. Use a piece of deal, otherwise the carving itself may be bruised. Of course a slight dent of the kind in oak may always be 'lifted' again by a few applications of spittle, the moisture of the saliva swelling the dent up.

"Most jobs can be best carried out on benches, but exception must be taken to figures and figure panels. These should never be laid on the flat, save for under cutting. A plant may be fixed vertically from the floor to the ceiling joists. Holes can be bored in this at convenient heights, and by means of a bench-screw—or more than one, if necessary—the statue or panel can be securely fixed level with the eye. Then the worker may bang away at it and see what he is doing.

"It is only thoughtless carvers who put finished or partly finished work down upon the floor, even for five minutes. There is always more or less dust upon the floor of even the best appointed shop, and soiled work is ever an abomination. Never let the glue pot touch the floor either. Dirty glue, of all things, is disgraceful. What looks worse than a black joint that suggests that somebody has been lining it with a lead pencil? Further, never use cheap glue. The more costly is the best and cheapest in the long run. The benches should be fixed firmly against the wall immediately under a continuous row of windows. It is well for the latter to be glazed with ribbed glass up to a level above the ordinary line of sight. This prevents the windows being looked through either by workmen or passers-by. Work naturally suffers if attention is diverted from it.

"It is a great mistake for a carver's bench to be placed, like a joiner's, in the midst of a shop; the light is then all wrong. The greatest number of wood carvers I ever saw at work together was at Pullman's car works, a dozen miles or so out of Chicago. It was in 1893, at the time of the World's Fair. There were fully 300 of them, all employed on piece-work, and the majority not earning more than they would have done in England. In the different shops there were two rows of continuous benches, one line of them arranged directly under the windows, and the other running parallel a few yards behind. I recollect those working in the rear complained bitterly how severely they were handicapped in regard to light."

Experience tells us that in winter time and on dark days it is always economical to keep plenty of artificial light burning in a carver's shop. At all times it "pays" better to light up half an hour too soon than five minutes too late. A man can always work better and more readily utilize an "inspiration" when the surroundings are cheerful. In dull weather it is well to keep the gas burning all day. As a rule, in a carver's studio when more light is required warmth is also desired. Gas gives light and makes warmth, and hence is better than electricity, for there is no warmth in the latter. When at work the carver should always wear a blouse —white by choice—and "sport" a clean one every Monday morning. Blouses not only greatly save

FIG 8.   FIG. 9.

the clothes, but are a pleasant distinction from the joiner's apron.

As I stated on a former page, the mallet made use of by the carver should have a round face, as shown in Figs. 8 and 9, though this is not absolutely necessary, as will be shown later on. The mallet, Fig. 9, is shown in operation in Fig. 10, which also shows the proper method of holding the chisel or gouge when the mallet is used.

Another shape of mallet is shown in Fig. 11, where some examples of tool holding are also illustrated, in which the proper position of the hands is shown while at work.

FIG. 10.

Except when using the mallet, hold the tool with both hands; in the right, the handle, the first and second fingers of the left hand resting on and guiding the tool an inch or so from the end. With both hands above the sharp edge, all danger of accident is prevented. When some force is required the mallet should be used. The handle of the tool should then be held firmly in the left hand, between the fingers and thumb, far enough from the end to escape the stroke of the mallet.

The best carvers' mallets are turned and made of apple-tree or hickory. A good average weight is two pounds. A larger one may be rather cumbersome for general work. Don't have too small a mallet; one weighing under a pound gives the impression of playing with work rather than doing it. Hence it is not suggestive of a diligent journeyman. In the old days mallets were oblong, like those used by joiners, although generally rounded off at the top. I remember when I went to the trade my first task was to make my own mallet of that shape. This I managed fairly well, the mortising for the handle being the most awkward part of the business to a mere novice; for

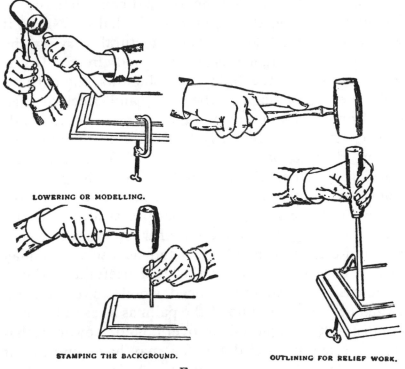

LOWERING OR MODELLING.

STAMPING THE BACKGROUND.

OUTLINING FOR RELIEF WORK.

FIG. 11.

there were no mortising machines in those days, or not at least in my own shop at Sheffield in the forties.

Although a mallet is not so necessary a tool to a wood carver as it is to the carver of stone, to whom it is an actual essential, its use cannot be too systematically cultivated. All rough-cut should be done with it, and bosses, cornices, and other work intended to be fixed at a height from the eye, should invariably be finished with the mallet. When engaged on these classes of work the mallet should never leave the carver's hand, for the cut left by the chisel with the mallet behind it is always the most effective when looked up at from the ground. Further, by the free and continuous use of the mallet the work is got over in half the time it would otherwise take. In architectural carving the great end to be attained is general good effect. If it is to be successful, the lights and shadows, the outlines and general grouping must be happy and effective when seen from the real point of sight, *i.e.*, the floor. Half a dozen strokes judiciously administered may make a really effective patera, whereas half a day's minute work upon a bench may produce something which, when placed in position upon the wall plate of a roof, will not only be disappointing but practically invisible.

It is a very general practice of wood carvers to use the half-closed palm of the hand as a sort of human mallet, and for light work this is a useful and wholesome custom. All experienced wood carvers have a large hoof in the middle of the palm as a result thereof. It must not be ignored or overlooked, however, that this practice, if carried too far, may have unpleasant or even dangerous consequences. As it is, few mature wood carvers can open their right hand quite straight. In course of time the habit causes the fingers to become rigidly bent inwards, although the flexor tendons and joints are unaffected. Subcutaneous division of the contracted bands sets the fingers free, but a relapse is nearly sure to occur. An eminent surgeon says, "There are quite half a dozen different operations in vogue for this deformity, but I never knew one which was really successful—that is to say, which resulted in a permanent cure."

Carvers sharpen their chisels and gouges quite differently from joiners and carpenters. These latter rub all from one side and get a hard beveled edge: the former get a thin, keen edge—on chisels and gouges alike—in the middle of the steel, rubbing from back and front. The best oilstones probably are known as Washita, and most favorite "slips" are those from Arkansas. The latter are, of course, for sharpening the concave insides of gouges, and are ground to various sweeps to fit them. After properly sharpening, the edges are "strapped" upon a buff leather—a soldier's belt makes a capital strap, rubbed in with crocus powder and tallow.

It is a singular but certain fact that soft wood requires keener edged tools to finish work cleanly with than hard wood. Thus deal or cedar must be carved with sharper tools than oak demands.

Besides his mallet and chisels a carver practically wants nothing but a hold-fast, screw, and a pair of calipers. Then he is set up, and can go anywhere, and—if the ability is in him—do anything.

A good carver rarely carries a lead pencil. He trusts to his eye. What will deceive a practical and well-trained optic will readily deceive the whole world. He never carries a rule under any circumstances. If by any chance he should require one for a minute or two, he borrows it from a joiner.

One of the most important branches of the carver's art is a knowledge of the proper methods employed in sharpening the tools he or she has to make use of. Sharp tools solve the mystery of clean cutting and good work. Great care should be taken that the edges of the tools do not knock or rub against one another. The good carver keeps his tools parallel with each other when not in use, or better still, he rolls them up in a slightly oiled cloth, having one layer of cloth between each tool.

Sharpening tools is to the wood carver what threading the needle is to the seamstress—a continual annoyance, yet not without its advantage, as it breaks in on a too long continued abstraction in work. Tools must be of very good quality and very sharp. Many tools which are brittle at first, at the edge, improve after this has been worn away. It will be necessary, while carving with one tool continuously, to touch it up on the hone about once in ten or fifteen minutes. It is hardly necessary to describe how tools are ground, for there is hardly a place in the world where there is not a tool seller, a carpenter, a smith or tinker who can show you the method. A grindstone and an oilstone are almost as necessary as tools. Carpenters' tools are sharpened on only one side, carvers' tools on both. The V tools and gouges are sharpened externally on the wheel and stones as chisels are. But the grinding on the inside is done with a bit of Arkansas oilstone, called a slip, ground or filed down so as to exactly fit the edge. Remember that to do this with only the stone and the tools is dangerous for the fingers. Therefore set the slip in a piece of wood, which may be screwed into a vise or laid on the table and held fast by nails.

After tools have been ground and had the first dull or wire edge removed, they must be set on an oilstone, which gives them greater keenness. They should then be stropped on a piece of leather. If there is no strop at hand a substitute may be found in the smooth surface of a planed pine board. It is difficult for a tyro to grind and set the V tool or gouges. Those who intend to carve should first of all learn to sharpen and set tools. It is by no means difficult to do this if they will only try. Gouges and chisels when purchased are beveled at the cutting edge. This bevel should always be preserved. When grinding the tools the gouges are held to the grinding stone at precisely the angle indicated and are moved backward and forward by the motion of the wrist across the grindstone, and at the same time are twisted between the thumb and fore-finger. This action preserves the curves, which must always be perfect. Little difficulty will be found in sharpening the chisels, as they are held to the grind-stone perfectly flat; yet they must be moved from one side of the stone to the other or you will work a groove in the stone in a very little time.

The oilstone is a tool that very few take proper care of. It is indispensable and therefore should be treated as carefully as the sharpest cutting instrument. Oil-stones should never be allowed to get clogged up with dirty, dried oil. They should be kept free from dust and grit. The best oilstone is one in a

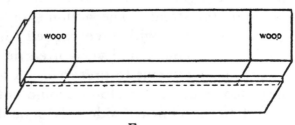

Fig. 12.

box that you can cover while working. Arkansas oil slips should be cared for in precisely the same way and wiped dry every time they are used.

A very good way to mount an oilstone is shown in Fig. 12. It is distressing to the trained mechanic to saunter through a workshop and see about half the oilstones on the bench worn hollow in the center like a sway-backed horse. This evil will be corrected if the stone is set in a block, as illustrated in the sketch, with pieces of hard wood about 1½ inches long at each end and flush with the face of the stone. This will enable the workman in sharpening his tools to whet over the ends of the stone as well as in the middle of it, thereby keeping it straight. Should the stone, after long use, show any hollow places, take a piece of No. 2½ sandpaper, laying it on a flat board, turn the stone face down and a brisk rubbing will soon put it in good shape again. If the board is well chalked before laying the sandpaper upon it, the latter will not slip whilst rubbing the stone.

When being honed, tools are held to the stone at the same angle or bevel as when being ground. The flat tools are rubbed up and down the stone, as if you were making a long figure 8. Hone on one side and then turn over to the other. The gouges are rubbed up and down the stone, twisting the tool between the thumb and fingers. These tools should not be pressed hard upon the stone. The action should be quick and light or the tools will have ragged edges, which are very hard to remove and very often destroy the curve you are most anxious to preserve. A gouge properly sharpened upon a flat stone should not want the slip applied to the concave side. It should only be used when there is a feathery edge. The constant use of the slip inside will spoil the curve, whether the stone fits it exactly or not.

When the outside of a gouge has been clearly rubbed up to the edge, the inside is to be rubbed out with a washita slip of the proper shape, as shown in Fig. 13, to the extent of half as much as the outside. The handle of the tool should be grasped in the left hand while its blade rests on a block of wood, or on the oilstone. Hold the slip between the fingers and thumb, slanting a little over the inner edge, and work it in a series of downward strokes, beginning the

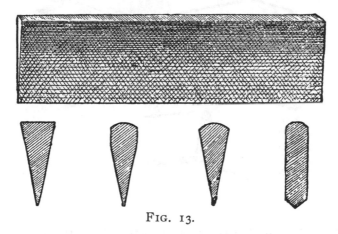

FIG. 13.

strokes at one corner of the gouge and leaving off at the other, as shown in Fig. 14. Strop the outside of the tool and test for burr, then lay the leather strap over the handle of another tool and strop the inside, repeating the operation until all burr has been removed, when probably the tool will then be ready for use.

The veiner requires the same kind of treatment, only this tool is no part of a circle in its section—having straight sides—only one-half must be done at a time, and it is well to give the straight sides one stroke or so in every half dozen, all to itself, to keep it in shape. Care must be taken with this tool, as it is easily rubbed out of shape. The inside must be finished off with the Arkansas knife-edged slip, one side at a time, as it is impossible to sweep out the whole section of these deep tools at one stroke. Stropping must follow as before, but as this tool is so small that the

FIG. 14.

leather strop will not enter its hollow, the leather must be laid down flat and the hollow of the tool drawn along its edge until it makes a little ridge for itself

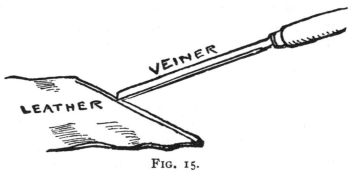

FIG. 15.

which fills the hollow and cleans off the burr; the method being shown in Fig. 15. If any burr adheres outside, a slight rub on the Arkansas stone will probably remove it.   When the edges of the tools begin to get dull, it often happens that they only require to be stropped, which should be frequently done.

A strop suitable for the carver's use may be made from a piece of good harness leather, or from an ordinary razor strop.   It is a good idea to glue a piece of good, suitable leather on the top or cover of the oilstone, which may be used for stropping flat chisels and many other tools.   Of course, a loose strop should always accompany a set of carving tools, whether the set number many or few pieces.

As the treatment of all gouges is more or less like what has been described, practice will enable the beginner to adapt it to the shape which requires his attention.   There remain only the V tools, the spoon tools and the macaroni which will require special attention.   The point of the V tool is so acute that it becomes difficult to clear the inside.   A knife-edged slip is used for this purpose, and it is well also to put a slip of wood to a thin edge, and after rubbing it with paste and oil, pass it down frequently over the point between the sides. Unless a very sharp point is obtained, this tool is practically useless; the least speck of burr or dullness will stop its progress or tear up the wood.   In sharpening it, the sides should be pressed firmly on the stone, watching it every now and then to see what effect is being produced.   If a gap begins to appear on one side, as it often does, then rub the other side until it disappears, taking care to bear more heavily on the point of the tool than else-where.   If the sides get out of shape, pass the tool along the stone, holding it at right angles to the side of the stone, but at the proper angle of elevation; in this case the tool is held near its end, between fingers and thumb.   Spoon tools must be held to the stone at a much higher angle until the cutting edge is in the right relation to the surface, or they may be drawn sidewise along it, taking care that every part of the edge comes in contact and receives an equal amount of rubbing.   These may be treated half at a time, or all round, according to the size and depth of the tool. However it is produced, the one thing essential is a long, straight-sectioned cutting bevel, not a rounded or obtuse one.   Strop the inside by folding up the leather into a little roll or ball until it fills the hollow of the tool.

For a small set of tools one flat oilstone and two slips will be found sufficient for a beginning, but as a matter of fact, it will be advisable, as the number of tools is enlarged, to obtain slips of curves corresponding to the hollows of all gouges as nearly as possible. Many professional carvers have sets of these slips for the insides of tools, varying in curves which exactly fit every hollow tool they possess, including a triangular one for the inside of the V tool.   The same rule sometimes applies to the sweeps of the outsides of gouges; for these, corresponding channels are ground out in flat stones, a process which is both difficult and laborious.   If the insides are dealt with on fitting slips, which may be easily adapted to the purpose by application to a grindstone, the outsides are not so difficult to manage, so that grooved stones may be dispensed with.

It is well to impress upon the beginner the extreme importance of keeping his tools in good order.   When a tool is really sharp it whistles as it works; a dull tool makes dull work, and the carver loses both time and temper.   There can be no doubt that the great technical skill shown in the works of Grinling Gibbons and his followers could not have been arrived at without the help of extraordinarily sharp tools—tools not merely sharpened and then used until they became dull, but tools that were always sharp and never allowed to approach dullness. Sharpening tools is indeed an art in itself, and like other arts has its votaries who successfully conquer its difficulties with apparent ease, while others are baffled at every point. Impatience is the stumbling-block in such operations.

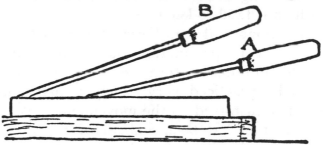

A - ANGLE FOR SOFTWOOD
- ANGLE FOR HARD WOOD
FIG. 16.

Those most painstaking people, the Chinese and Japanese, according to all accounts, put magic into their sharpening stones; the keenness of their blades being only equaled by that of their wits in all such matters of delicate application. To make a good beginning is a great point gained. To carefully examine every tool, and at the expense of time correct faults of management, is the only way to become expert in sharpening tools.

When tools are to be used in soft woods their bevels will require to be longer than when for use in the harder woods. I show both angles in Fig. 16, which will give the reader some idea of the requirements in both cases.   Lay the flat of the tool on the stone at an angle of about 15 degrees, with the handle in the hollow of the right hand, and two fingers of the left pressed upon the blade as near to the stone as possible. Then begin rubbing the tool from end to end of the stone, taking care not to rock the right hand up and down, but to keep it as level as possible on the blade with the left hand, to keep it well in contact with the stone.   Rocking produces a rounded basil or bevel edge, which is fatal to keenness.

Practice alone will familiarize the muscles of the wrist with the proper motion, but it is important to acquire this in order to form the correct habit early. It should be practiced very slowly at first, until the hands get accustomed to the movements.   When one side of the tool has been rubbed bright as far as the cutting edge, turn it over and treat the other in the same way.   Carvers' tools, unlike joiners', are rubbed on both sides, in the proportion of about two-thirds outside to one-third inside.   When a keen edge has been formed, which can easily be tested by gently applying the finger, it should be stropped on a piece of stout leather.   It will be found, if the finger is passed down the tool and over its edge, that the stoning has turned up a burr.   This must be removed by stropping on both sides alternately.   A paste composed of emery and crocus powders mixed with grease is used to smear the leather before stropping; this can either be procured at the tool shop or made by the carver.   When the tool has been sufficiently stropped, and all burr removed, it is ready for use, but it is as well to try it on a piece of wood first and test it for burr, and if necessary strop it again.

Before we leave this tool, however, we shall anticipate a little and look at it after it has been used for some time and become blunt. Its cutting edge and the bevel above it are now polished to a high degree, owing to friction with the wood. We lay it on the stone, taking care to preserve the original angle (15 degrees). We find on looking at the tool after a little rubbing that this time it presents a bright rim along the edge, in contrast with the gray steel which has been in contact with the stone. This bright rim is part of the polished surface the whole bevel had before we began this second sharpening, which proves that the actual edge has not yet touched the stone. We are tempted to lift the right hand ever so little, and so get rid of this bright rim (sometimes called the "candle"); we shall thus rub away all the steel behind it. We do this, and soon get our edge; the bright rim has disappeared, but we have done an unwise thing and have not saved much time, because we have begun to make a rounded edge, which, if carried a little further, will make the tool useless until it is reground. There is no help for it, time must be spent and trouble taken in sharpening tools; with method and care there need be very little grinding, unless tools are actually broken.

A good way of testing the keenness of edge on a tool is to try it on a piece of soft pine, cutting *across* the grain, when, if the tool is properly sharpened, a clean cut, without any tearing of the grain, will be the result.

Before commencing a piece of carving I should recommend the student to spend an hour or so in getting in order those tools likely to be required, and unless the work is of an intricate character, a dozen or eighteen will be sufficient.   When in use, the tools are placed on the bench with the blades pointing towards the worker, and owing to the slight difference in the size and sweep of many of them, it is advisable to know the tools by the handles, so as to be able to at once pick up the tool required.

In case the beginner has unground tools supplied him, and must rely on himself or the friendly aid of a carpenter to do the grinding, the difference between the edges of an ordinary cutting tool, such as a chisel, and of carvers' tools must be noted.

What might be a very good edge for ordinary joinery would not suit the carver.   Tools for carving must taper much more gradually, so that they have a more knife-like edge than a joiner's or cabinetmaker's tools.   Figs. 17 and 18 represent approximately the

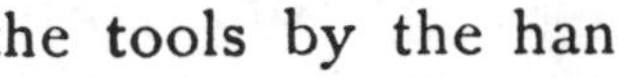

FIG. 17. 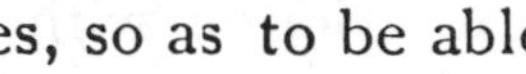   FIG. 18.

two kinds of edges, that required on carving tools being the thinner of the two.   If the tools are ground by any one unaccustomed to the wants of the carver this difference must be insisted on, for however keen the actual cutting edge may be, satisfactory work cannot be done unless the tools have a long-tapered edge. It is therefore at least as important to see that the grinding or initial sharpening is correctly done as the subsequent sharpening on the oilstone.   Though this, as well as the former, requires skill, there is less risk of spoiling a tool by a novice, and if he cannot get a carver to do what is necessary he need not hesitate to do the sharpening himself.   Indeed, the sooner he learns to do so the better, as tools are constantly requiring to be sharpened, and the practice of getting an expert to do this whenever needed is not always convenient. Even if it is, it is far better that the carver should be able to keep the tools in order for himself. If the tools are new, even if they are said to be "sharp," it is often a tedious job to get really satisfactory edges. A good deal of patience may be necessary, but any trouble is justified by the result. When once the tools are right, it is a comparatively easy matter to keep them so. To prevent misunderstanding, it is well that the beginner should know that the edge should be as "sharp as a razor." An edge that would do for even a sharp knife would not do for carving. The tools must cut quite cleanly without tearing or bruising the wood. The work should look as if it had been cut, not as if it had been worried or "gnawed by rats."

By the oilstones all roughness left by grinding must be rubbed down, and no sharp angle must be left where the bevel and the straight part of the blade unite.

Tools should be sharpened on both sides, as in Fig. 17, and not only as in Fig. 18. This especially applies to chisels, as in gouges the difference is hardly so decided. When sharpening chisels, care must be taken to keep the bevel straight, and not to let the edge get rounded off.

The sharpening of gouges presents greater difficulty than in the case of flat tools, and the rule may be stated as being that they should be ground on the outside and sharpened on the inside. It is, however, necessary to use the oilstone on the outside first, to remove the roughness left from grinding, and occasionally afterwards to keep the edges in condition. Great care must be taken with gouges that the edge across from corner to corner is straight, so that if the tool be placed with its edge against a flat surface the whole of the edge will touch. If anything, the corners may be slightly rounded off, but on no account must the edge be irregular. Unless care be taken, such an edge, faulty though sharp, will result from either bad grinding or sharpening.

The best directions the beginner can have are that the sharpening should be done evenly, all parts of the edge being sharpened equally. This, although somewhat difficult in practice, may be done by beginning at one end of the stone, against which a corner of the gouge rests, and gradually turning the tool as it is drawn along the stone to the other end, the tool being all the time at right angles to the stone, as before stated.

This applies to the outside of the gouge. The sharpening proper must be done on the inside, and for this the small slips already referred to must be used. Many amateurs find a difficulty in using these, as the pieces of stone are short, and being held in one hand while the tool is held in the other, unless manipulated properly cuts are apt to occur. To avoid mishaps of this kind various devices have been suggested. None of them, however, is so satisfactory as the ordinary way, about which there should be no risk if the worker will proceed as directed on a previous page. In other words, to repeat, rub the stones against the tool, and not *vice versa*. There is then no danger of the carver cutting himself by the stone slipping off the tool. This, with slight modifications, is the method adopted by all practical carvers, and is far better than any amateurish plan of fixing the slip and rubbing the tool against it.

In the case of ordinary cutting tools the stone produces a sufficiently keen edge, but not on carving tools. They must be finished off by stropping, much in the same way that a razor is stropped. Much has been written at various times about preparing strops for carvers, but they cannot do better than follow the suggestions given.

Still, any piece of buff leather may be used. It should be prepared by rubbing in a little preparation composed of grease and some very fine powder, such as emery flour, putty powder, the finest pumice powder, or even dust. This latter, from its fineness, is the best when the strop has been matured, but with it alone some time is required to get the strop into condition. Emery powder, even when in its finest form of flour, cuts away the tool rather too much if freely used, and as a happy medium between the two extremes there is nothing superior to jewelers' rouge. Whether this or anything else is used it is just rubbed into the leather with a little grease of any kind. At most tool shops a "razor paste" is sold in small, collapsible tubes, and does well for the carver.

The strop must never be absent when the carver is at work, for it is in constant requisition, and it is a bad plan to neglect its use. The older it gets the more highly it is esteemed generally, and if the tools are properly used an occasional rub with the strop will keep their edges in such condition that the oilstone will seldom be required.

Some carvers are in the habit of letting the tools all get dull and then having a general sharpening up; it is necessary to say that this is not a good one, and the carver should make a practice of keeping his tools constantly in the best possible condition.

Before concluding on this subject it may be well to

give the novice a reliable test by which it may be ascertained whether the edges of the tools are sufficiently sharp. It is very simple, and consists merely in cutting *across* the grain of a piece of soft wood, pine being generally used for the purpose. If the tools cut the wood cleanly, leaving a smooth surface, they are all right. If, however, there is any appearance of roughness from the grain of the wood having been torn through rather than cut, the edges of the tools are not sharp enough, and the carver should not be satisfied with them until they will stand the above test.

It may be noted that an edge may be sharp enough to cut a hard wood easily and yet not cut a soft one clearly. Hence the recommendation to test tools on pine. If they cut it properly they may be used on any kind of wood.

I do not know that I can add anything to the foregoing in the way of sharpening the tools mentioned; there will, however, be other cutting tools we will meet before the volume is completed, the care and sharpening of which will be discussed when we reach the proper place.

It will now be in order to consider the methods in general use to hold the work in position while being operated on. Those who cannot command a workroom and regular bench may be assured that excellent work can be done on an ordinary table provided it is substantial enough to be rigid, or can be fixed in some way as already indicated. It can hardly be too strongly insisted on that unless the table or bench be sufficiently firm to resist the thrusts against the tool when carving, good work cannot be done. Therefore, those who have not a perfectly firm bench will do well to confine themselves to small carving, such as can be done without moving or shaking the bench or table.

It may be as well to say here that even a table with a good top which one would not wish to injure, such as a dining table, may be used by the carver.

The next important point to be considered is the method to be adopted for holding the wood while it is being carved, for it must be known that both the carver's hands are engaged with the cutting tool. It is useless to attempt to hold the wood with one hand and to carve with the other.

Although the wood must be rigidly held so that it cannot slip about on the bench top, it is also desirable that it should be easily released and fixed in an altered position, for it is often necessary to do so to get at particular parts.

A good deal depends on the work itself as to what is the most convenient way of securing it to the bench, and it is impossible to give directions which shall apply equally to each and every case. The carver must use his own discretion and consider what facilities are available. To guide him, the following suggestions will be sufficient. If an ordinary joiners' bench is used, it will be provided with a bench vise, which may be useful occasionally, but it is so rarely indispensable to the carver that nothing more need be said about it.

For flat work, *i.e.*, incised or chip carving on the flat, by far the most convenient appliance for holding the wood is the "bench hold-fast," shown in Fig. 19. It consists of a round bar of iron which passes through a hole made for the purpose in the bench. The arm is hinged on to it and is raised and depressed by means of a screw working on the top of the bar, fixing the wood firmly to the bench in the required position. To use it, the long portion is passed through the hole in the bench top, the panel is placed under the end of the curved portion, and the screw turned. To prevent the panel being damaged by the iron, a piece of waste wood can be inserted between them. The "wood carvers' screw," shown in Fig. 20, is another useful appliance of recognized merit for all kinds of carving, and indispensable to the professional carver.

FIG. 19.

It is very simple, consisting only of a strong iron screw, which is passed through a hole in the table, into which it should fit somewhat tightly; it is then screwed up into a similar hole bored in the body of the carving and secured by an iron nut under the table which, when screwed home, fixes it down to the table as firmly as required; the iron may penet ate into the wood as far as the nature of the carving will permit, the farther the better, as the greater hold it takes so much the more firmness will be insured. Great care must be taken on first boring the hole to guard against the carving and also to see that the boring is straight.

FIG. 20.

It will often be convenient to have a block of wood with a hole in it for the screw to pass through underneath the bench. This block not only prevents the wood about the hole in the bench being worn away, but saves a good deal of time and trouble otherwise.

The screw, although it may be used for panel carving, is specially useful for work which cannot well be kept in place by the "hold-fast."

Apart from the cost, the chief objection—from an amateur's point of view—to both hold-fast and screw is the necessity of having a work bench or table used exclusively for such, on account of the hole in the top. This, of course, cannot be allowed on a table, and other means must then be devised for holding the work. That these are not altogether of a makeshift

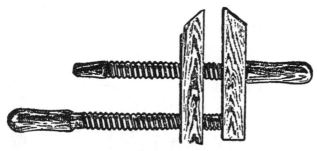

Fig. 22.

character may be inferred from the fact of professional carvers occasionally using them.

As the protection of the table top is often an object, it may be well to suggest that this can be sufficiently provided for by having what may be called a false top. The size of this piece must depend on that of the wood, which it may be assumed is a panel, being carved. Provided it is larger, nothing more is wanted, so that a piece of boarding 1 inch thick and a few inches larger than the panel will do very well.

To hold this board to the table the ordinary wooden handscrews, as in Fig. 22, may be used, and if the

carving is sufficiently far from the edge of the wood
they do well.   The manner of its working is shown in
Fig. 23.   There is, however, the objection that the

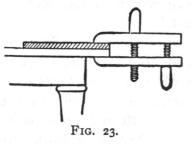

ends of the screws, being
above the table, may be in
the way of the carver.   Unless the work is very large,
small iron cramps, of which
there are many varieties, are
preferable; one of them is
shown in Fig. 24, and it will

FIG. 23.

be seen that by having the screw downwards there
is very little projection above, and even this may be
done away with by cutting
a small space in the top
of the carving board. The
method of its application
is shown in Fig. 25.   It is
seldom that one cramp
will hold this firmly, but
as they are very cheap it
is not a serious matter to
have two or three of them.
If possible, the board
should be placed at a
corner of the table, as it is
then so much easier to secure it.

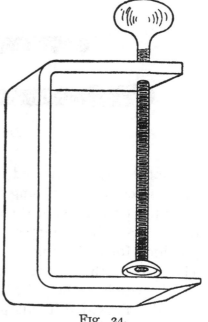

The work being carved
may be fastened to the
board or simply held to it

Fig. 24.

in any position that may suit the carver.   In the former
case the position of the board must be altered,
and to do so is not always convenient.   Which is

the better plan to pursue, the carver must decide for himself.

If the panel is to be fixed to the board, it may be managed by means of screws or glue. The screws are merely driven through from below the board into the panel. This way does very well if the screw holes are not a disfigurement, and if the panel is sufficiently thick for the screw points to hold in it without there being any risk of the carving tool coming in contact with them. If the screws are inadmissible, glue must be used; but if the two surfaces are directly glued together it will be difficult, if not impossible, to get them apart again without injury. The way to manage is to glue them together with a piece of paper between. Thus a piece is stuck on the panel and this is then glued to the boards. When the work is done, by inserting a knife blade between the two pieces the paper splits and they come

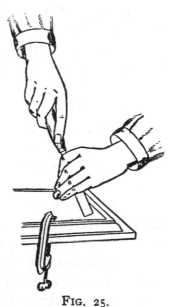

FIG. 25.

apart. Almost any kind of paper may be used, but none is better than newspaper. It is seldom necessary to glue the entire surface, as a touch here and there, at the discretion of the worker, is generally sufficient.

It may be as well to remind the beginner that it is sometimes useful, even when the hold-fast or carvers' screw is used, to have a piece of wood fastened on behind the carving; for instance, when the former might damage the carving if laid directly on its face, or when the panel is so thin that the screw could **not** be used with it.

When it is desired to have the carving movable on the board, the devices that may be used are almost endless in their modifications, and only a few can be suggested.

Three or four screw nails may be driven into the board, close to the edges of the panel, so as to prevent its moving. The heads of the nails clamp the panel down sufficiently. This method seems more cumbersome than it really is, for it is seldom necessary to remove and refix more than one or two of the screws whenever the position of the panel is altered.

A more fanciful method, and one which has some advantages over the foregoing, is to bore a series of holes in the lower board and cut pegs to fit them. With a sufficiency of holes and a little management, it will be found easy to fix the panel in any desired position with four or five pegs. These should be of sufficient stoutness to resist the thrusts of the carving tools, and must project over the board, so that the panel is against them. A fresh hole can easily be made whenever required.

A more workmanlike plan, and one that is even simpler than the above, is to have one or more wooden catches shaped somewhat as Fig. 26. They can

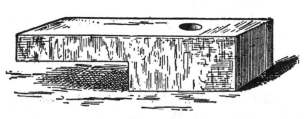

FIG. 26.

be made as required, and should be of some tough hard wood. The part cut away for the thickness of the panel should be a trifle less than this, so that on tightening the screw the carving is firmly held.

If loosening and tightening the screw each time the panel has to be moved is objected to, the alternative of having the opening deeper than the thickness of the panel may be adopted. The panel then fits in quite loosely, and can be easily fastened with a wedge or two driven in above the panel. Putting in the wedge below the panel would have the effect of tightening up, but the panel might not lie firmly, *i.e.*, it might give too much under the pressure of the tools. It is in just such instances that the discretion of the carver will come into play. What may be the easiest and best method in certain circumstances may be awkward and unsatisfactory in others, and so much is this the case that it may almost be said that an expert carver has no hard and fast regulations for fixing work, but varies his methods as occasion requires. All he requires is that the work shall be held sufficiently firm to allow of the tools being used efficiently, and that alterations in position can be made easily and without loss of time. If the learner will remember these general principles he will be saved some perplexity in knowing how to hold any piece of carving he may be engaged on.

An exceedingly good device to fasten on a table or bench is shown in Fig. 27; it has the advantage of compactness and is made to use on any table without injuring it; for this object the three rests on the table and the top of the little movable square, C, are covered with baize; when screwed up close to the table the stand is perfectly secure and it is a plan which I can recommend from my own experience; should it, however, be desirable not to go to this expense, any old table will answer the purpose if it can be fixed so as to be perfectly firm.   This device is a little costly, but is well worth all that may be paid for it.

In addition to the above tools, carvers occasionally use one called a "router," or what the carpenter calls

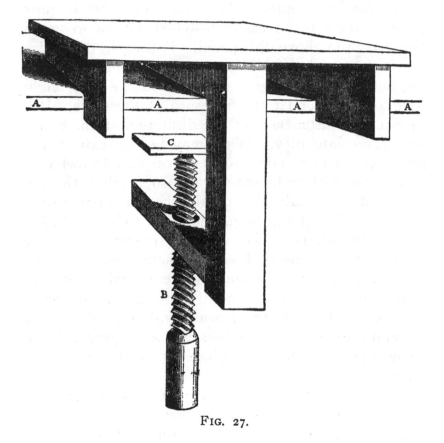

FIG. 27.

an "old hag's tooth," Fig. 28.   This is a kind of plane with a narrow, perpendicular blade.   It is used for digging or "routing" out the wood in places where it is to be sunk to form a ground.   It is not a tool to be recommended for the use of beginners, who should learn to make sufficiently even backgrounds without the aid of mechanical contrivances. Carvers also use the "rifler," which is a bent file. This is useful for very fine work in hard wood, and also for roughly ap-proximating to rounded forms before finish-ing with the tools.

A few join-ers' tools are very useful to the carver and

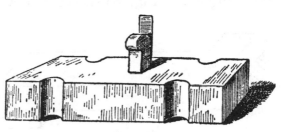

FIG. 28.

should form part of his equipment. A wide chisel, say about 1¼ inches wide, a small iron "bull-nose" plane, and a keyhole saw will all be helpful and save a lot of unnecessary la-bor with the carving tools, also one or two ordinary saws for cut-ting off and ripping

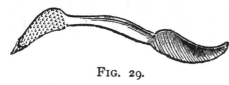

FIG. 29.

stuff. The regular carpenter, of course, will have all these tools, but as this work is prepared for all sorts of people, many of whom may not be carpenters, general instruc-tions must be given.

The "rifler" or bent file is shown in Fig. 29. It is used

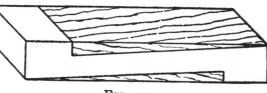

FIG. 30.

for cleaning out or smoothing surfaces where the flat tools cannot be used. These may be bought at the hardware store, or files may be softened and bent to shape and then hardened again.

The bench hook is an indispensable article to the wood carver, whether amateur or professional, its purpose being to hold the wood while the shoulders, etc., are being cut.   Fig. 30 shows a piece of wood marked out ready for shaping into the "hook," the grained portion having to be cut away. A suitable length is 12

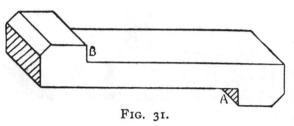

FIG. 31.

inches, the other sizes being 2 inches wide by 1½ inches thick.

The complete hook is shown in Fig 31, and in use it is laid across the bench, clipping the sides of the latter at A, while the wood to be cut rests against B, which receives the thrust of the saw.

CHAPTER II

WOODS

After tools, the materials on which to use them stand next in importance. In the choice of these the worker must be guided by the nature and style of carvings he chiefly affects; speaking generally, oak is the best wood for large subjects, and ebony or box-wood for small, minute work; but walnut, whitewood, chestnut (both horse and Spanish), mahogany and basswood are all suited to the purpose, while sandal-wood, apple, pear, holly, cypress, fig and lemon tree, being hard and fine grained, may all be used with good effect, according to the style and size of the carving and other circumstances. English oak is much to be preferred to home-grown wood, which is of a hard and tough nature, and liable to knots, which are a great impediment to the carver and from which most foreign oak is comparatively free. These oaks may be known by the close and smooth grain and somewhat gray tinge; our wood being coarser grained and of dingy color. Oak is especially suited to decorate work in a library or large hall, for ecclesiastical purposes and for imitation antique carving.

Spanish chestnut and mahogany may be classed next after oak for carvings which, though large, require a great amount of finish. Of mahogany there are two very distinct kinds, one of them being comparatively soft—it is known as bay-wood or Honduras mahogany—the other kind is harder and darker and known

as Spanish; many of the works of the great Gibbons
are carved in this wood, though many of them are in
the softer and less durable whitewoods.

Black walnut is a wood always in favor. It is of
moderate hardness and cuts cleanly. Other walnut
wood is not so suitable, though occasionally used.

Sycamore, whitewood, holly and woods of that
nature, being white or cream colored, are only suited
to that special style of carving the beauty of which
depends on great purity of coloring—such, for instance,
as a minute basso-relievo after a picture, models of
figures in imitation of ivory, groups of birds, or delicate
foliage, such as we sometimes see exhibited in proof
of the artist's skill—but all these woods, unless pro-
tected by glass, soon lose their extreme whiteness and
with it their chief beauty; therefore they are little used,
excepting for the trifling purposes we have just
mentioned. The woods of the apple and pear trees
are, from the hard texture and fine grain, exceedingly
pleasant to work, but their value as productive trees
renders them rare, and the occasional deep-colored
veinings sometimes interfere with the design. Boxwood is equally hard and fine grained, and is far
superior in uniformity of color, which is a rich yellow.
The great bar to the free use of all these hard woods,
apart from any difficulty in carving them, is the
difficulty of procuring them in pieces of any size, for
they are mostly of small growth, rarely attaining to
more than 10 or 12 inches in diameter.

Ebony or black wood is very suitable for small
carvings of every description, whether for use or
ornament, the deep black color and the hardness and
fine texture of grain giving it, when polished, the
appearance of black marble. This wood is also some-

what difficult to procure in large blocks, for it rarely arrives here in logs of any size that are not more or less riven and spoilt by cracks and flaws—"shakes," as they are termed in timber merchants' parlance. There are two kinds of ebony, the green and the black, but for carving purposes there is little or nothing to choose between them, though the black is capable of taking a finer polish, its only drawback being an occasional white or red streak. These are rare and can be easily obliterated by applying a little ink to the spot after the carving is finished.

Sandalwood, from the texture, beautiful color (a rich yellow brown), and the delicious scent which is familiar to everybody, is especially suited for small carvings. The superabundance of oil, which emits so delightful a fragrance, causes it also to take a beautiful polish merely by rubbing it slightly with the hand. The best sandalwood is brought from India and Ceylon. It also, like ebony, is difficult to procure in sound pieces. It is sold, as are the most valuable woods, by weight. Small pieces are cheaper than large ones in proportion, unless they are prepared and squared to any given size, and then they are far more expensive, as in the course of preparation two or three logs may perhaps be cut up and spoilt before one can be found without flaw, and of course this waste is taken into account and charged for by the wood merchant. Ebony and boxwood are sold in the same manner. Each little piece is valued for the smell, even the chips and sawdust being treasured by some people to burn on the hearth to scent the room.

Ordinary woods—oak, walnut, mahogany, white-wood, maple and others—are generally sold by measurements and can be bought in quantities from a timber merchant, or if only a small piece be wanted, from a carpenter or a cabinetmaker. The hard woods, if the carver live in the country, are more difficult to procure. Occasionally a carpenter with a good stock may be found, and he may be willing to sell some, but this is often an expensive way; therefore it would be wiser to buy from a regular dealer when possible.

It is needless to say that the longer all kinds of wood are kept before being used so much the better seasoned they will be. We would, therefore, advise all who can conveniently do so to lay in a stock of those woods which they are in the habit of using. It must, however, be stored up with care, excessive heat and all damp being avoided. If possible, saw out the piece required a short time before the actual carving is commenced, as then any little defect which on first being cut would be imperceptible will be detected. This is a very wise precaution, as nothing is more disheartening and provoking than to be obliged to cast aside work commenced, and on which perhaps time and labor have been expended, on account of the material turning out worthless.

It will generally be found that wood got from a dealer of repute is seasoned, but this is not always the same as being dry; hence the necessity of the foregoing caution.

Pine is generally regarded as being too common for carving purposes, but there is no reason why it should be altogether neglected. It is cheap and soft, so that for the beginner it is perhaps the best wood that can be got. If care be taken in selection, it can be got free from knots in sufficiently large pieces. Red or yellow pine should be used, not spruce, which is very knotty and unpleasant to work.

Whitewood is another good and cheap wood which has come into considerable use the last few years. It cuts cleanly and is remarkably free from knots or flaws of any kind. When suitably stained it is very like walnut in appearance.

As ivory has a fascination for many amateurs, it should be pointed out that this material is very costly, and that the difficulty of carving it properly is so great that it is quite unsuitable till considerable proficiency has been acquired. Various imitations are made, but the best of them is xylonite, which so far as appearance is concerned is not to be distinguished from the real thing. To prevent disappointment, the variety known as ivory grain should be got. It cuts fairly easy, the only objection to it being that it very quickly blunts the tools.

The following woods may be considered as having an intermediate place between soft and hard: sycamore, beech and holly. They are light-colored woods, and very useful for broad, shallow work.

Of the hard woods in common use the principal kinds are oak, walnut, and occasionally mahogany. Of oak, the English variety is by far the best for the carver, being close in the grain and very hard. It is beyond all others the carver's wood, and was invariably used by them in England during the robust period of mediæval craftsmanship. It offers to the carver an invigorating resistance to his tools, and its character determines to a great extent that of the work put upon it. It takes, in finishing, a very beautiful surface when skillfully handled, and this tempts the carver to make the most of his opportunities by adapting his execution to its virtues. Other oaks, such as Austrian and American, are often used, but they do not offer quite the same tempting opportunity to the carver. They are, by nature, quicker growing trees and are, consequently, more open in the grain. They have tough, sinewy fibers, alternating with softer material. They rarely take the same degree of finish as the English oak, but remain somewhat dull in texture. Good pieces for carving may be got, but they must be picked out from a quantity of stuff. Chestnut is sometimes used as a substitute for oak, but is better fitted for large scaled work where fineness of detail is not of so much importance.

Italian Walnut. This is a very fine-grained wood, of even texture. The Italian variety is the best for carving; it cuts with something of the firmness of English oak and is capable of receiving even more finish of surface in small details. It is admirably suited for fine work in low relief. In choosing this wood for carving, the hardest and closest in grain should be picked, as it is by no means all of equal quality. It should be free from sap, which may be known by a light streak on the edges of the dark brown wood.

European walnut has too much "figure" in the grain to be suitable for carving. Our own walnut is best fitted for sharply cut, shallow carving, as its fiber is caney. If it is used, the design should be one in which no fine modeling or detail is required, as this wood allows of little finish to the surface.

Mahogany, more especially the kind known as Honduras, is very similar to our walnut in quality of grain; it cuts in a sharp caney, manner. The "Spanish" variety was closer in grain, but is now almost unprocurable. Work carved in mahogany should, like that in American walnut, be broad and simple in style, without much rounded detail.

It is quite unnecessary to pursue the subject of woods beyond the few kinds mentioned. Woods such as ebony, sandalwood, cherry, briar, box, pear-tree, lancewood and many others are all good for the carver, but are better fitted for special purposes and small work. As this book is concerned more with the art of carving than its application, it will save confusion if we accept yellow pine as our typical soft wood and good close-grained oak as representing hard wood. It may be noted in passing that the woods of all flowering and fruit-bearing trees are very liable to the attack of worms and rot.

No carving, in whatever wood, should be polished. I shall refer to this when we come to "texture and finish."

CHAPTER III

SOMETHING ON THE GRAIN OF WOOD AND OTHER IMPORTANT MATTERS

It is curious to imagine what the inside of a young enthusiast's head must be like when he makes his first conscious step towards artistic expression. The chaotic jumbles of half-formed ideas, whirling about in its recesses, produce kaleidoscopic effects, which to him look like the most lovely pictures. If he could only learn to put them down! Let him but acquire the technical department of his art and what is easier than to realize those most marvelous dreams? Later in his progress it begins to dawn upon him that this same technical department may not be so very obedient to his wishes; it may have laws of its own which shall change his fairy fancies into sober images not at all unlike something which has often been done before by others. But let the young soul continue to see visions; the more the better, provided they be of the right sort. We shall in the meantime ask him to curb his imagination and yield his faculties for the moment to the apparently simple task of realizing a leaf or two from one of the trees in his enchanted valley.

With the student's kind permission we shall, while these lessons continue, make believe that teacher and pupil are together in a classroom, or better still, in a country workshop, with chips flying in all directions under busy hands.

I must tell you, then, that the first surprise which awaits the beginner, and one which opens his eyes to a whole series of restraints upon the freedom of his operations, lies in the discovery that wood has a decided grain or fiber. He will find that it sometimes behaves in a very obstinate manner, refusing to cut straight here, chipping off there, and altogether seeming to take pleasure in thwarting his every effort. By and by he gets to know his piece of wood—where the grain dips and where it comes up or wriggles—and with practice he becomes its master. He finds in this, his first technical difficulty, a kind of blessing in disguise, because it sets bounds to what would otherwise be an infinitely vague choice of methods.

We shall now take a piece of yellow pine, free from knots, and planed clean all round. The size may be about 12 inches long by 7 inches wide. We shall fix this to the bench by means of two clamps, or one clamp and a screwed block at opposite corners. Now we are ready to begin work, but up to the present we have not thought of the design we intend executing, being so intent upon the tools and impatient for an attack upon the silky wood with their sharp edges.

The illustration, Fig. 32, gives a clue to the sort of design to begin with; it measures about 11 inches long by 7 inches wide, allowing a margin all round. The wood should be a little longer than the design, as the ends get spoiled by the clamps. This little design need not, and indeed should not, be copied. Make one for yourself entirely different, only bearing in mind the points which are to be observed in arranging it, and which have for their object the avoidance of difficulties likely to be too much for a first effort. These points are somewhat to this effect: the design should be of leaves, laid out flat on a background, with no complication of perspective. They should have no undulations of surface. That is to say, the margins of all the features should be as nearly as possible the original surface of the wood, which may have just the least possible bit of finish in the manner I shall describe later on. The articulation of the leaves and flower is represented by simple gouge cuts. There should be nothing in the design requiring rounded surfaces. The passage for tools in clearing out the ground between the features must not be less than ¼ inch; this will allow the $\frac{3}{16}$ inch corner grounder to pass

Fig. 32.

freely backwards and forwards. The ground is supposed to be sunk about $\frac{3}{16}$ of an inch.

As you have not got your design made, I shall, for convenience' sake, explain how Fig. 32 should be begun and finished. First having traced the full-size design, it should be transferred to the wood by means of a piece of blue carbon paper. Then with either the veiner or V tool outline the whole of the leaves, etc., about ⅛ inch deep, keeping well on the outside of the drawing. Ignore all minor detail for the present, blocking out the design in masses. No outline need be grooved for the margin of the panel at present, as it should be done with a larger tool. For this purpose take gouge No. 6 ¼ inch wide (see Figs. 37 and 38), and begin at the left-hand bottom corner of the panel, cut a groove about $\frac{1}{16}$ inch within the blue line, taking care not to cut off parts of the leaves in the process; begin a little above the corner at the bottom and leave all a little below that at the top. The miters will be formed later on.

In this operation, as in all subsequent ones, the grain of the wood will be more or less in evidence. You will by degrees get to

FIG. 33.

know the piece of wood you are working upon, and cut in such a way that your tool runs *with* the grain and not *against* it; that is to say, you will cut as much as possible on the up-hill direction of the fiber This cannot always be done in deep hollows, but then you will have had some practice before you attempt these.

Now take chisel No. 11 and with it stab into the grooved outline, pressing the tool down perpendicularly to what you think feels like the depth of the ground. The mallet need not be used for this, as the wood is soft enough to allow of the tools being pressed by the hand alone as shown, but remember that the force must be proportioned to the depth desired and to the direction of the grain; much less pressure is wanted to drive a tool into the wood when its edge is parallel with the grain than when it lies in a cross direction; small tools penetrate more easily than large ones, as a matter of course, but one must think of these things or accidents happen. (See Figs. 33 and 34.)

When you have been all round the design in this way with such gouges as may be needed for the slow and quick curves, get the wood out nearly down to the ground, leaving a little for finishing. Do this with any tool that fits the spaces best; the larger the better. Cut across the grain as much as possible, not along it. The flat gouge No. 1 will be found useful for this purpose in the larger spaces, and the grounders for the narrow passages. This leaves the ground in a rough state, which must be finished later on.

FIG. 34.

Now take gouges Nos. 2, 3, 4, 5, 6, 7 and chisels Nos. 10, 11, 12, and with them cut down the outline as accurately as possible to the depth of the ground, and, if you are lucky, just a hair's breadth deeper. In doing this make the sides slope a little outwards towards the bottom. If the gouges do not entirely adapt themselves to the contours of your lines, do not trouble, but leave that bit to be done afterwards with a sweep of the tool, either a flat gouge or the corner chisel used like a knife.

Now we have all the outlines cut down to the depth of the background, and may proceed to clear out the wood hanging about between the design and the ground all round it. We shall do this with the "grounders," using the largest one when possible, and only taking to the smallest when absolutely necessary on account of space. This done, we shall now proceed to finish the hollow side of the panel and make the miters. Again, take No. 6 gouge and drive a clear hollow touching the blue line at end of panel and reach-

FIG. 35.

ing the bottom of the sinking, i.e., the actual ground as finished, see a, Fig. 36. To form the miter at top of left-hand side of panel, carry the hollow on until the tool reaches the bottom of the hollow running along the top; as soon as this point is gained, turn the tool out and pitch it a little up in the way shown at c, Fig. 36, in which the tool is shown at an angle which brings the edge of the gouge exactly on the line of the miter to be formed. Beginning as it does at b, this quick turn of the handle to the left takes out the little bit of wood shown by dotted lines at *b*, and forms one-half of the miter.   The cross grain cut should be done first, as in this way there is less risk of splintering. Now repeat the process on the long grain side of the panel, and one miter is in a good way for being finished.

A word now about these sides of sunk panels. They always look better if they are hollowed with a gouge instead of being cut square down.   In the first case they carry out the impression that the whole thing is cut from a solid piece of wood, whereas when they are cut sharply down they always suggest cabinetmaking, as if a piece had been glued on to form a margin.

We have now got the work blocked out and the ground fairly level, and we are ready to do the little carving we have allowed ourselves. Before we begin this I shall take the opportunity of reminding you that you must be very careful in handling your tools; it is a matter of the greatest importance, if the contingency of cut fingers or damaged work is to be avoided.   The left hand in carving has nearly as much to do as the right, only in a different way.   Grasp the chisel or gouge in the left hand with the fingers somewhat extended, that is, the little finger will come well on to the blade and the thumb run up towards the top of the handle; the wrist meanwhile resting on the work.   The right hand is used for pushing the tool forward, and for turning it this way and that, in fact does most of the guiding.   Both hands may be described as opposing each other in force, for the pressure on the tool from the right hand should be resisted by the left until almost a balance is struck and just enough force left to cut the wood gently, without danger of slipping forward and damaging it or the fingers. The tool is thus in complete command, and the slightest change of pressure on either hand may alter its direction or stop it altogether. Never drive a tool forward with one hand without this counter resistance, as there is no knowing what may happen if it slips. Never wave tools about in the hand, and generally remember that they are dangerous implements, both to the user and the work. Never put too much force on a tool when in the neighborhood of a delicate passage, but take time and eat the bit of wood out mouse-like, in small fragments.

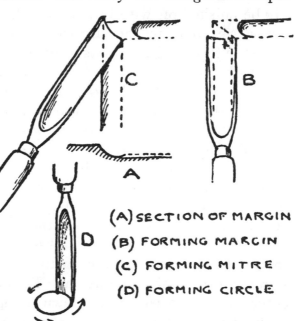

(A) SECTION OF MARGIN
(B) FORMING MARGIN
(C) FORMING MITRE
(D) FORMING CIRCLE

FIG. 36.

Now we are ready to finish our panel. Take the grounders, according to the size required, always using the biggest possible. Keep the tool well pressed down, and *shave* away the roughness of the ground, giving the tool a slight sideway motion as well as a forward one. Work right up to the leaves, etc., which, if cut deep enough, should allow chips to come away freely, leaving a clear line of intersection; if it does not, then the upright sides must be cut down until the ground is quite clear of chips. Grounder tools are very prone to dig into the surface and make work for themselves; sharp tools, practice, and a slight sideway motion will prevent this. Tool No. 23 is useful in this respect, its corners being slightly lifted above the level of the ground as it passes along. Corners that cannot be reached with the bent chisels may be finished off with the corner chisel.

Now we come to the surface decorations, for the carving in this design consists of little more. This is all done with the gouges. Generally speaking, enter the groove at its widest end and leave it at the narrowest, lowering the handle of the tool gradually as you go along, to lift the gouge out of the wood, producing the drawing of the forms at the same time. A gouge cut never looks so well as when done at one stroke; patching it afterwards with amendments always produces a labored look. If this has to be done, the tool should be passed finally over the whole groove to remove the superfluous tool marks—a sideway gliding motion of the edge, combined with its forward motion, often succeeds in this operation. To form the circular center of the flower, press down gouge No. 5 or 6 gently at first and perpendicular to the wood. When a cut has been made all round the circle, work the edge of the tool in it, circus-like, by turning the handle in the fingers round and round until the edge cuts its way down to the proper depth. (See Fig. 36, A.)

Carve the sides of the leaves where necessary with flat gouges on the inside curves, and with chisels and corner chisels on the outside ones. These should be used in a sliding or knife-like fashion, and not merely pushed forward. Finish the surface in the same manner all over between the gouge grooves and the edges of the leaves, producing a very slight bevel as

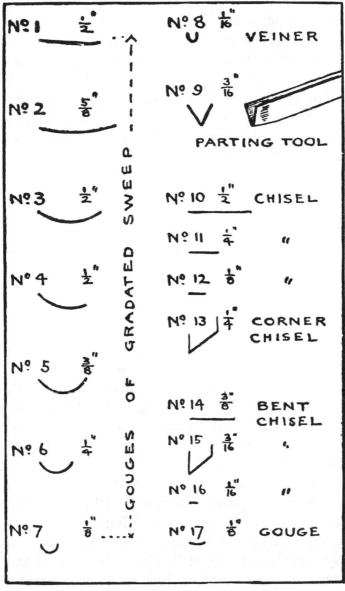

FIG. 37.

in section *a*, Fig. 34, and this panel may be called finished.

Fig. 35 is another suggestion for a design, upon which I hope you will base one of your own as an exercise at this stage of your progress.

The gouges, chisels and other tools referred to in the foregoing are shown and numbered in Figs. 37 and 38. The sizes of each tool are also given, so that the learner will have no difficulty whatever in picking out the exact tool he may require to complete the work as shown in Figs. 32 and 33. These two illustrations, with the tools and their sections shown, will be of great use to the learner in many ways

We now leave this subject and take up the question of "chip" or "spot" carving, which I hope to be able to explain and illustrate in such a manner as to satisfy the learner in every particular.

"CHIP" OR "SPOT" CARVING, AND ALL ABOUT IT

"Chip" or "spot," or "notch" carving as it is sometimes called, is by no means new as a recreation; no doubt many readers are aware that highly ornamental effects are to be got from it and that the work, though simple, is extremely interesting. It is not, however, generally known how much may be done with a solitary tool made for the purpose. As a rule, the learner is told to use carving tools of the ordinary kind. These are all very well in their way, but to use them properly requires a bench or table of some kind and a fair amount of practice. Even when done with them, chip carving as compared with ordinary carving is easy, but is simpler still when done with the tool referred to. It is not a new one, but somehow or other it has escaped proper recognition of its powers.

Those who have written on the subject of chip carving
have alluded to its existence, but as a rule that is all,

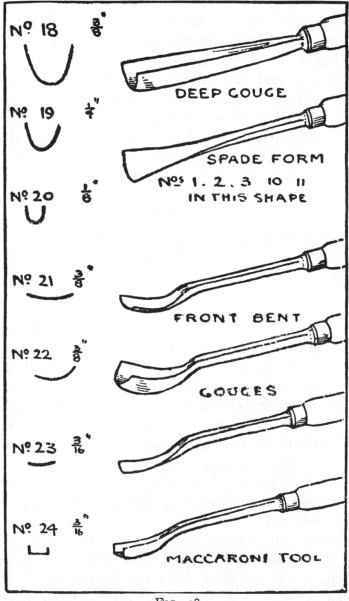

FIG. 38.

although it is *the* tool for chip carving, and easy though the work may be, a few directions will help the novice.

Perhaps it will be well to explain what chip, or notch carving as it is often called, is as distinguished from the ordinary kind. Briefly, it is a method of ornamenting surfaces generally, but not necessarily, flat, by cutting variously shaped notches or hollows in them. These, being arranged in an orderly manner, and mostly of a geometrical pattern, form the decoration. The cuts, it should be stated, are nearly always made on the slant from opposite directions, so that the bottom of each notch, instead of being flat, is merely the angle formed by the two sides. As we proceed further this will be more easily seen; in

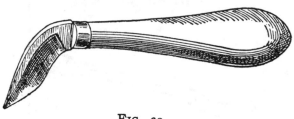

FIG. 39.

the meantime let the novice make with the point of a penknife two cuts, say ¼ inch or less apart, and of any angle, though on the surface of one piece of wood and sloping downwards towards each other. Whatever the angle at which the cuts are made, they must meet. Now make two cuts at a similar slant of the ends of the long one, and a rectangular notch will be the result. This is the germ of all chip carving, the pattern depending on the curves, size and general arrangement of the notches.

The tool with which this carving may be done consists of a hooked blade fitted in a handle, as shown in Fig. 39, the blade being about 1½ inches long. These knives are not generally kept at tool shops, but **may** be obtained from many dealers. In shape different blades vary slightly, as in Fig. 40; the former, being more rounded off and thinner towards the point, is to be preferred to the latter.

The carver does not require to support the work on a table or bench, though he may do so if desired. Generally it is just as easy to hold the wood in one hand and work the knife with the other. Instead, therefore, of having the work always lying flat on the table, it can be moved about to suit the kind of cut being made. Herein lies the great convenience of the knife compared with the ordinary carving tools. To the majority of amateurs it will feel more familiar in the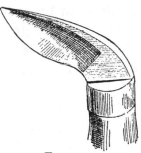

FIG. 40.

hand, from its resemblance to an ordinary knife. One way of holding it is with the handle firmly grasped in the right hand, and the first joint of the forefinger curved over the back of the blade. This is especially useful when the wood is being held in the other hand, but unless the right hand is moved as the cut proceeds, does not give much freedom of action when the work is on a table. Another way of holding it, and one by which both power and freedom of action is gained, is to grasp the handle with all four fingers, not resisting them in the work. The thumb gives the necessary support to afford steadiness to the cut, and allows of a cut of considerable length being made. Great power may also be gained by resting the thumb against the edge of the piece of wood being carved, if this is not too large. The second and third methods will be found exceedingly useful when cutting curves, which are the most difficult notches at first.

In order to make a curved notch easily, the knife should be so held that the elbow is well away from the carver's body, so that the full sweep can be given with the blade.

Another method, requiring both hands, is to hold the knife in the right and press against the back of the blade with the left thumb. It is sometimes a relief to have recourse to this plan, especially when cutting straight lines, and it will be understood the work must be on some support.

These are all typical methods of making the cuts; but it must not be inferred that the knife may not be held in any other way. Any in which the carver finds he can get the most command over the tool will be the right way, and after a very small amount of practice no regard need be consciously paid to the way in which the knife is held; it will be held naturally in the best way to do the work intended.

As with other carving tools, the edge cannot be too sharp, so that no amount of trouble should be spared to get it into good condition and to keep it so. The carver should always work with a strop at hand, and give the blade a rub or two whenever its cutting powers show the smallest sign of giving way. An ordinary razor strop does as well as anything, and it will not be long before the novice discerns the increased comfort to himself and benefit to the work of keeping the knife well stropped. To save him needless trouble, it may be well to say that nearly all the cutting is done with the ½ inch or so of edge nearest the point, so that the chief attention should be paid to this part. A blade with a back thick close up to the point is not as easy to cut with as one which is judiciously tapered.

With regard to the handle, all we would say about it is that though its polished condition when new may look very nice, the polish is rather an objection than otherwise. A firmer grip is got on an unpolished surface, and this will be found more noticeable when the hands are moist with perspiration. Mere good looks in this should give way to utility, and if desired the polish can easily be removed by scraping or with glasspaper. The novice may again be cautioned on no account to use glasspaper on the wood to smooth it before carving, or till the carving is finished; if he does, it will be found that the blade gets dull "in no time" from the small grits which have worked into the wood from the paper.

This style of carving is one of the simplest, but is by no means of modern origin, as its development may be traced to a source in the barbaric instinct for decoration common to the ancient inhabitants of New Zealand and other South Sea Islands. Technically and with modern tools it is a form of the art which demands but little skill, save in the matter of precision and patient repetition. As practiced by its savage masters, the perfection of these two qualities elevates their work to the dignity of a real art. It is difficult to conceive the contradictory fact that this apparently simple form of art was once the exponent of a struggling desire for refinement on the part of fierce and warlike men, and that it should, under the influence of polite society, become the all-too-easy task of æsthetically minded school girls. In the hands of those warrior artists, and with the tools at their command, mostly fashioned from sharpened fish bones and such like rude materials, it was an art which required the equivalent of many fine artistic qualities, as such are understood by more cultivated nations. The marvelous dexterity and determined purpose evinced in the laborious decoration of canoe paddles, ax handles, and other weapons, is, under such technical disabilities as to tools, really very impressive. This being so, there is no inherent reason why such a rudimentary form of the art as "chip" carving should not be practiced in a way consistent with its true nature and limitations. As its elemental distinctions are so few and its methods so simple, it follows that in recognizing such limitations we shall make the most of our design. Instead, then, of trusting to a forced variety, let us seek for its strong point in an opposite direction, and by the monotonous repetition of basket-like patterns win the not-to-be-despised praise which is due to patience and perseverance. In this way only can such a restricted form of artistic expression become in the least degree interesting. The designs usually associated with the "civilized" practice of this work are, generally speaking, of the kind known as "geometric," that is to say, composed of circles and straight lines intersecting each other in complicated pattern. Now the "variety" obtained in this manner, as contrasted with the dignified monotony of the savage's method, is the note which marks a weak desire to attain great results with little effort. The "variety" as such is wholly mechanical; the technical difficulties, with modern tools at command, are felt at a glance to be very trifling; therefore such designs are quite unsuitable to the kind of work, if human sympathies are to be excited in a reasonable way.

An important fact in connection with this kind of

design is that most of these geometric patterns are, apart from their uncomfortable "variety," based on too large a scale as to detail.   All the laborious carving on paddles and clubs, such as may be seen in museums, is founded upon a scale of detail in which the holes vary in size from $\frac{1}{16}$ to something under $\frac{1}{4}$ inch their longest way, only in special places, such as borders, etc., attaining a larger size; such variety as the artist has permitted himself being confined to the *occasional* introduction of a subtle change in the proportion of the holes, or an alternate emphasis upon perpendicular or horizontal lines.

As a test of endurance and as an experimental effort with carving tools, I set you this exercise. Fig. 41 you will find a pattern taken from one of those South Sea carvings which we have been considering. Now take one of the articles so often disfigured with childish and hasty efforts to cover a surface with so-called "art work," such as the side of a bellows or the surface of a bread plate, and on it carve this pattern, repeating the same shaped holes until you fill the entire space. By the time you have completed it you will begin to understand and appreciate one of the fundamental qualities which must go towards the making of a carver—namely, patience; and you will have produced a thing which may give you pleasant surprises in the unexpected but very natural admiration it elicits from your friends.

Having drawn the pattern on your wood, ruling the lines to measurement, and being careful to keep your lines thin and clear as drawn with a somewhat hard pencil, proceed to cut out the holes with the chisel No. 11 on your list, $\frac{1}{4}$ inch wide. It will serve the purpose much better than the knife usually sold for this kind of work, and will be giving you useful practice with a very necessary carving tool. The

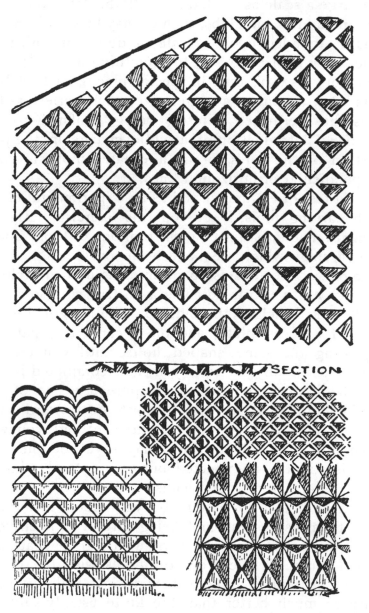

FIG. 41.

corner of the chisel will do most of the work, sloping it to suit the different angles at the bottom of the holes. Each chip should come out with a clean cut, but to ensure this the downward cuts should be done first, forming the raised diagonal lines.

When you have successfully performed this piece of discipline, you may, if you care to do more of the same kind of work, carry out a design based upon the principles we have been discussing but introducing a very moderate amount of variety by using one or more of the patterns which are from the same dusky artists' designs and cannot be improved upon.

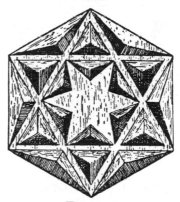

FIG. 42.

To satisfy the present requirements of fashion, however, it is necessary that I should show a number of the prevailing styles of carving in this kind of work, so I offer as a start a simple design in which the notches are of a fair size and so do not include too many small curves.

To any one who can use a pair of compasses and a rule, or has any knowledge of geometry, the difficulty of drawing the designs on wood will be so trifling as not to be worth considering. As the designs I offer show the shading, and consequently the inner or bottom angles, and not merely the outlines on the surface, it will be well for the learner to know that he need draw only the latter; the angles indicated by the others form themselves naturally as the cuts are made. Thus Fig. 42 represents a regular hexagon, containing two triangles and a six-corner star in the center as shown in the design. The lines at the bottoms of the shaded pockets or notches are clearly discernible, but need not be drawn on the wood; it is merely the outline as shown in Fig. 43. An examination of Fig. 43 will clearly show how the various lines are set out, and,

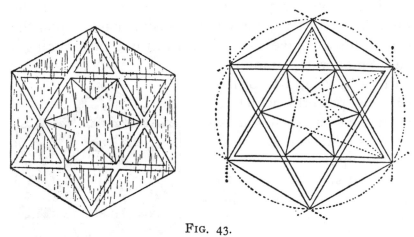

FIG. 43.

supposing the design is now transferred to the wood with carbon paper, fairly will represent the drawing before carving is commenced.

In making the cuts the precise angle at which the blade is inclined to the wood is not of much consequence, but it should be as uniform as possible. The hand will almost insensibly become accustomed to cutting at the same slope, or so nearly the same that the difference in depth of the same sized notches in any piece of work is not noticeable. As far as possible, the cuts should be made cleanly and to the required depth at once. This, however, is often impracticable, and it is necessary to make more than one cut to get to the bottom. When this has to be done, the utmost care should be taken that the second and succeeding cuts are exactly at the same angle as the first, for if not the notch, or rather that particular side of it, will show a ridge wherever the cut has been unequal, instead of being quite smooth. The irregularity may be pared away afterwards, but to do this is a waste of time and the work seldom looks so clean as if done properly at first.

Perhaps the novice may be inclined to think that it would be easier to begin paring away a notch from the center, gradually increasing the size till the outline is reached. At first it may be so, but facility will not be obtained in doing the work, and he should begin, as indicated, boldly on the outline.

From the point of the knife penetrating further than it need at the bottom of the notches, it will often be observed that there is a kind of slight burr turned up. This may easily be removed if the work is small and for close inspection, otherwise it may be disregarded. The cuts themselves do not require any attention.

When the carving has been done, the work may be cleaned off with glasspaper used in the ordinary way over a cork block. It must be remembered that the notches themselves cannot be worked on with the paper, which only cleans up the surface of the wood. The dust will work itself into the cuts referred to in the previous paragraph so that they will be barely distinguishable. To make the work as clean as possible it should be finally brushed with a stiff brush, and may then be regarded as complete.

As to the wood, very little need be said. At first it is not advisable to use any hard kind, and none is more suitable than a piece of good, sound, clean pine; it is soft and cuts cleanly. Another good kind to begin with is American whitewood, though pine is on the

whole to be preferred. In the course of time it
assumes a pleasant, warm tone. It or any other wood
may be varnished, for French polishing is out of the
question; but it is a matter of opinion whether the
appearance is improved, as size causes the surface to
swell and roughen, and as there is no means of rubbing
them down again it must not be used. The varnish
must be applied instead till it does not sink. Stains
are also objectionable for the same reason as size. If
any must be used, let them be mixed with spirits or

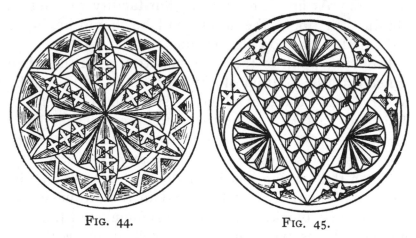

FIG. 44.   FIG. 45.

turps instead of water, though even then the result is
seldom pleasing, as more is absorbed by the end grain
than elsewhere, giving the work a dirty, patchy look.
A less objectionable way is to treat it with Aspinall's
or some similar enamel. Instead of painting all over
with one color, the notches may be picked out with
various tints, and if these are judiciously chosen very
pleasing effects may be obtained. In the same way
bronze paints of different tints may be used, though at
some risk of the decoration tending rather to barbaric splendor than to artistic taste.

When sufficient progress has been made to enable it to be worked, there is no wood better than oak. Though hard, it is not unpleasant to cut if a nice piece has been got. It is not, however, suitable for very small work, for which a fine, close-grained wood should be chosen. Chip carved oak looks remarkably well when darkened either by oiling or by fumigation, or by a combination of both, and then wax polished. Varnish destroys its beauty and gives it a coarse, commonplace appearance.

HOW TO HOLD THE KNIFE.

MAKING THE FIRST CUT.

Some very fine effects can be obtained by a division of the circle to the designs shown in Figs. 44 and 45.

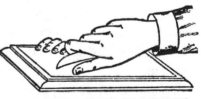

HOW TO HOLD THE KNIFE FOR SECOND CUT.

The various methods of cutting these ornaments with the knife shown in Figs. 39 and 40, are shown in the illustrations given in Fig. 46, where the knife is seen at work and the position of the hand during the cutting process.

HOLDING THE PARTING TOOL.

FIG. 46.

In using this tool, first draw a few lines parallel with the grain of the wood, following exactly one of these lines with the parting tool, holding the tool in the same position and exerting an equal amount of strength throughout. When you have succeeded in cutting a line clean, straight and uniform in width, draw several across the grain in different directions. The tool will meet with more resistance when cutting across the grain, but a few trials will give confidence and successful results. Curves should also be practiced in this manner. First large ones, afterward the arcs of very small circles may be attempted. Never "wriggle" the tool in the wood.

Do not attempt to remove too much wood at a time. Cut clean; whenever possible, with the grain. Never break or pry off any pieces of wood. Work slowly and carefully at first. Leave no rags, jags or fragments. Clear out completely every corner. Get your work as smooth as possible with whatever tool seems best to use. Let every stroke of the chisel, gouge or parting tool be made and regulated with purpose and design.

The use of sandpaper is not recommended as the best method of smoothing work. Sharp tools, careful cutting, with the skill acquired from practice, will soon render other aids unnecessary.

The wood to be carved must be smooth, close-grained, firm, but not hard; well seasoned, not kiln dried. Much practice renders the carver indifferent to the hardness of the wood. But the amateur is easily discouraged by wood that requires great strength to cut, when a skillful use of the mallet has not been acquired.

An ideal wood on which to chip carve is sweet gum,

containing no streaks of white. Gum wood is beautiful in grain, light brown in color. The path of the tool through it is smooth and glossy. This wood must be properly secured against warping when used in cabinet work.

Sycamore is of a delicate cream tint, flecked with brown. It has the same advantages as gum wood, but must also be secured against warping. Black walnut is dark brown in color, taking a beautiful finish. Oak is very hard, and should only be used after the beginner has had some practice upon other woods.

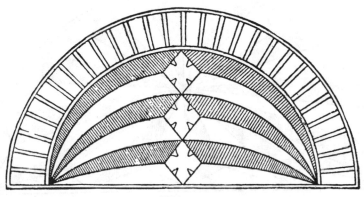

FIG. 47

White maple is very even in grain, almost as white as holly and as hard as oak. Poplar, pine, whitewood are easy to work and take stain quite readily, and may be used for small articles, but for large pieces or for furniture woods less easily scratched should be used.

I show herewith a number of designs the learner may try his hand upon, as they offer no particular difficulty either of design or construction, being of the simplest sort. In the ornament shown in Fig. 47 the whole scheme is a semicircle, with a series of radial grooves on its outer rim. The lines forming the boundary are simply incised work, cut in the wood V-shaped, as are also the radial lines and the inside boundary lines, hence the figure so far is made of simple V lines chased in the wood with the V tool only.   The lozenge-shaped ornaments are marked off and left flush, and the crescents are then worked to them, the center lines as marked being left as a hollow ridge sunk below the surface.

Another piece of chip carving is shown in Fig. 48. In this case lines show the raised ridge, while others

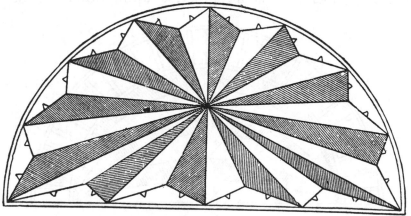

FIG. 48.

show hollow or sunk ridges.   There is a depression on the ends of the wings as deep as the sunken ridge. The boundary lines show a raised portion of the work. This is an extremely simple pattern.

Fig. 49 shows a circular ornament complete, made on the same lines as Fig. 48, only more of it.   The two triangles are left flush, as shown, and are pebbled with a punch made for the purpose.

Fig. 50 shows a corner of a picture frame or a border for a glove box or lady's workbox; it is worked on the same lines as Fig. 49, with the exception of the pebbled or padded work, which is easily wrought and as easily laid out.

These examples are presented, not because they are

FIG. 49.

considered good carving or work that will likely be called for, but because they make good examples for practice, and if spoiled do not mean much, but in working them the operator will soon find the "use of his hands," or, in other words, he will become accus-

tomed to the use of his tools and able to guide them
with accuracy—two very important acquisitions.

Chip carving offers an abundance of opportunities to

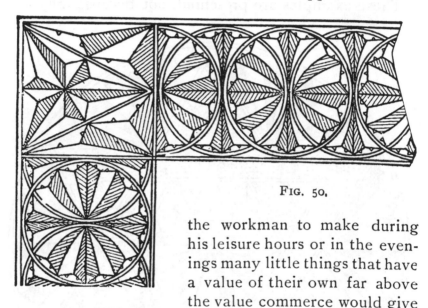

FIG. 50.

the workman to make during
his leisure hours or in the even-
ings many little things that have
a value of their own far above
the value commerce would give
them, such as cuff boxes and collar boxes for himself,
a glove and trinket box for his mother, his wife, his
sister, or his lady friends and thereby serving them a

FIG. 51.

good turn and getting practice and experience in the
management of his tools and the methods of work. A
continuation of these examples will be proceeded with.

The ornamentation shown in Fig. 51 is a little more complex than previous examples, but I do not think the workman will find it difficult to form or to execute, as

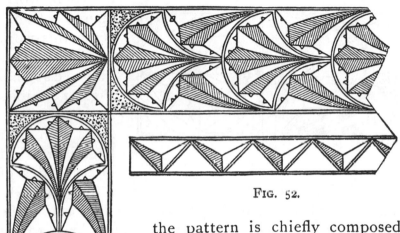

FIG. 52.

the pattern is chiefly composed of parts of circles and straight lines. I would advise the beginner not to attempt making his work too deep until he becomes well accustomed to the patterns and has a good com-

FIG. 53.

mand of his tools. A low relief or a shallow pattern is much easier to work and does not require so much labor to execute; though, of course, it is not as effective as would be a pattern worked in deeper; nevertheless, work of this kind when well done has a very pleasing effect. Another example of this kind and I am done, as I think there will be sufficient to enable

FIG. 54.

the young workman to both execute this work and form his own designs. Fig. 52 exhibits a couple of designs suited for borders of boxes, sides of tables, tabourets and similar pieces of furniture. In almost all of the examples shown the cuts forming the ornaments are beveled from the surface down to the bottom of the work, so that the bottom lines are formed by the two sides or slopes making a junction at the lowest point of the work where the two sides meet. This is a peculiar characteristic of chip carving.

FIG. 55.

The border shown in Fig. 53 looks complicated, but is really very simple both to lay out and to make, and when finished is quite striking.

The two examples shown in Fig. 54 may be used for corners of box lids or other similar work with good results; the same may be said in regard to the three-sided ornament shown in Fig. 55, which is well adapted for corners of any kind. The circular ornament shown in Fig. 56 is suggestive and can be made to suit many situations.

FIG. 56.

The series of designs shown in Figs. 57, 58, 59, 60, 61, 62 and 63 may be found useful for many purposes, and they offer suggestions to the designer for other designs of a similar kind. The borders 61, 62 and 63 will be made available for the edges of lids, tabouret tops and like work.

In Fig. 64 I show eight simple examples of borders, all in chip carving, that can be made to do service in many situations. These borders are of a kind that are easily made and when made can readily be adapted to a thousand and one purposes which are not necessary to mention here.

With the six examples of finished work shown in Fig. 65 I will close the chapter on "Chip Carving,"

FIG. 57.

but before doing so I must apologize to all my readers for the length of time I have devoted to this subject, as I am aware that most expert carvers look with contempt on this branch of the art. My excuse, however, for toying with this particular branch of the art so long is, that this book is intended more for young beginners than for the finished artist, and to these young people chip carving has a sort of fascination, because of its simplicity, that the more intricate work

FIG. 58.

does not possess, and offers an inducement to them to become carvers, an event that would not happen if the more difficult branch was the only one they could commence with.

Of the six examples shown in Fig. 65, two of them are circular. These should be roughed out in a lathe

and the center cut out to receive a porcelain plate or
other china ornament. The jewel box may be obtained

FIG. 59.

all ready to carve from any wood turner. The plate
frame is really a picture frame, the wooden rim being

FIG. 60.

turned with the center cut out to receive a valuable plate or other china; the frame is then carved in any design determined upon.

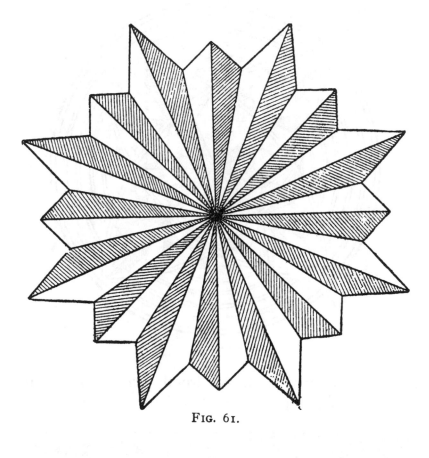

Fig. 61.

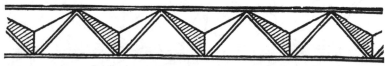

Fig. 62.

With this we leave this branch and start operations on another and a similar one, namely, "Flat Carving."

CHAPTER IV

FLAT CARVING

This style of carving is something similar to chip carving, the only difference being that in flat carving leaves, fruit, foliage and other objects, to which may be added lace or strap work in Celtic style, are introduced.

This mode of carving is very much in vogue among the Turks, the Persians and Afghans.

FIG. 63.

An example of Turkish work in this style is shown in Fig. 66. This is supposed to be the top of a tabouret. The work is laid out in a similar manner to chip carving, the dark lines all being one width and the light portions being removed.

In this kind of work care must be taken not to have one portion of the work deeper than another, as the

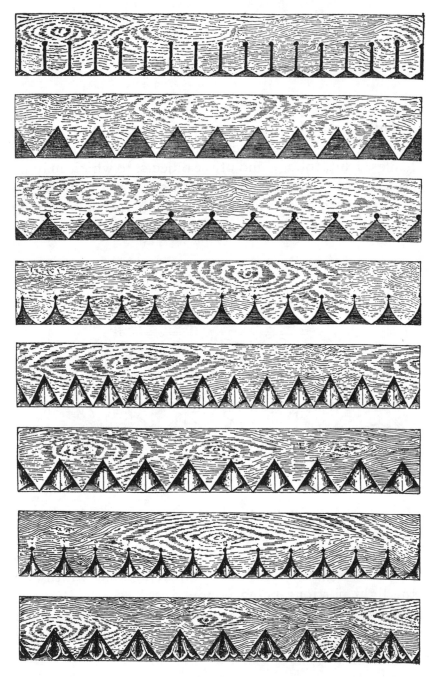

Fig. 64.

eye will detect any inequality in the surface beneath the raised ornaments. When finished, the work should look as though it had grown there.

Fig. 65.

A good pattern to practice on is shown in Fig. 67, which may all be done with the V tool and the narrow chisel.   In laying this out on the wood the lines should be formed with a good black pencil to the width

FIG. 66.

required.   Then cut away all the black lines, the thin lines being taken out with the V tool and the thicker ones either with a gouge or narrow chisel.

Under this head, "flat carving" with a background may be considered, as the difference only consists in the fact that the groundwork is pebbled, padded or stamped.

The three examples shown in Figs. 68, 69 and 70 exhibit designs with simple scratched backgrounds. This scratching is done with a tool which has a diamond point, and which, when used, is "drawn" towards the workman—never pushed.

FIG. 67.

These examples will give the young learner an opportunity to learn to use the left as well as the right hand, an acquirement that must be obtained before the operator can become an expert carver. The accomplishment is not difficult, and should be acquired after a month or so of practice. People who are left-handed, when beginning to carve, experience no difficulty whatever when learning the art in making use of the right hand.

The two corner ornaments shown in Figs. 71 and 72 are very simple in outline and have punched backgrounds. They may be formed of thin pieces of wood and nailed or screwed in position where wanted. If screwed in place the heads of the screws should be plated or oxidized to harmonize with the color of the wood employed.

The border Fig. 73 is a very good example and one that the learner can easily follow, as the curves, with the exception of the little beads, are of good sized sweeps and can be easily wrought.   The bottom or

FIG. 68.

background is padded with a small irregular-shaped punch, and the work is made as irregular as can be, but care should be taken not to have the punchings in too close clusters; they should spread over the grounds pretty evenly, so far as markings are concerned.   This applies to all sorts of padding on backgrounds, unless ornamented punches are used.

A simple leaf design is shown in Fig. 74, which may all be executed in the flat with the exception of the groove in the center of the leaf, which should be veined with the V tool. The padding on the ground is somewhat d i ff e r e n t from that on some of the previous examples, as the closer punchings near the base of the leaves answer as a shading and tend to bring out the design in greater apparent relief.

The design shown in Fig. 75 is a little more pretentious than most of those shown in this chapter, and is designed for a center-piece suited to box lids, d r a w e r fronts, tabourets, or any similar work. While being quite effective in its own peculiar way, it will not be found diffi-

FIG. 69.

cult to execute. The padding of the background may be as shown, or ornamented punches may be used for the work, according to the taste of the worker.

Fig. 70.

The initial letter shown in Fig. 76 is somewhat more
elaborate than the preceding examples, more particularly in the padding, where several kinds of punches
have been used.   This trick is often resorted to in
fancy flat carving, and if the work is executed in oak,

walnut, teak or
other dark wood
and then simply
oiled over with
raw linseed oil
it is very effec-
tive and rich looking.
This is a fine example, and
if made about twice the
size as shown here and the
edges of the raised work
veined as shown, it be-
comes a refined piece of work and would
assuredly be admired.

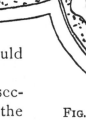

FIG. 71.

I have before shown a series of sections for punches and described the
manner of making them, but in order
to give the student the widest range possible within the

FIG. 72.

FIG. 73.

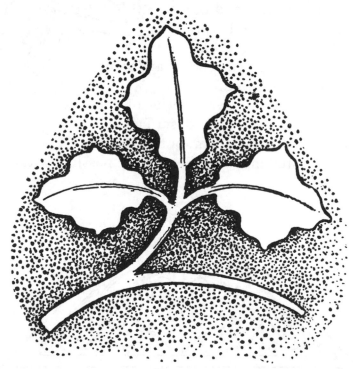

FIG. 74.

limits assigned to this book I illustrate another series of punches or stamps, most of which the learner may be able to make himself. These are shown in Fig. 77, where twelve different shapes are illustrated.

Perhaps a few words regarding the use of these

FIG. 75.

stamps may not be out of place at this juncture. It should be borne in mind that results from the use of these stamps are always better in hard wood than in soft wood, owing to peculiarities of the grain. The pounding of the stamp should always be even. If hit hard in some places and gentle in others, the stamping or

FIG. 76.

padding will show uneven on the background, more
particularly in the softer woods.   A regular and even
tap on the end of the punch
or stamp can be given readily
after a little practice.   Hard
wood requires a heavier blow
to make an impression than
soft wood, and this must always be considered.   It is a

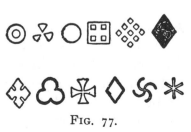

FIG. 77.

good plan to try one's hand on a piece of wood of the sort we are working before commencing to pad the groundwork of the carving, and then the right depth of impression may be regulated by the quality of the tap given the punch.

Before leaving this subject I deem it necessary to submit a few elaborate designs in this style of carving which are taken from existing examples. I show these in Figs. 78, 79 and 80, and, although all classed under the style Jacobean, the examples represent three distinct species of decoration and may therefore be considered separately. Fig. 78 is in reality four panels embodied in one design, i.e., if each quarter is taken separately and repeated it will make a distinct panel. Whilst thus differing in minor points, the designer intended that these panels should be used together in the same article. This element in the design brings out an important feature in ancient as well as modern Jacobean, viz., general uniformity and balance of parts, combined with pleasing variety of

FIG. 78.

detail. It would have been easier for the designer to have struck off one portion and to have written on the corner, "Repeat four times," but such a multiplication would not do for the author of these sketches.   In

Fig. 78 we, moreover, find a conventional t r e a t- m e n t o f plant forms which has been so much cultivated since our artist set the fashion, an element which is the distinguishing characteristic of modern Jacobean carving. It will be seen that the four ideas embodied in this one panel are equally suitable for a perpendicular or horizontal position. In Fig. 79 we get a more ancient

FIG. 79.

specimen of carving in the same style. It is a little study that serves to mark the connecting link between the Elizabethan and the later phases of English Renaissance. The influence of "strap work" originals is most evident in Fig. 79, and the design should be useful as showing how essentially decorative such a "motif" is when properly handled. The handsome

entablature set forth in Fig.
80 marks the period when
Jacobean was rich in characteristic detail.   In the center panel, with its Tudor rose
and surrounding strap work,
we are reminded of Eliza-
bethan, while the ground-
work from which it stands
out is more Jacobean in treatment.   The presence of those
ever recurring e n r i c h e d
bosses or pateras, the scroll
corner and egg and tongue
margin, all denote the source
of the design.   In these examples the sections will be
found sufficiently indicated
to guide the carver in making
a full-sized working drawing
from them to the desired
proportions.   Of late years
carving in relief has not been
so much cultivated as it ought
to have been.   To save expense the decorative spirit
of Jacobean has been omitted,
and what was left of old
lines has been badly made up
and often dubbed "Early
English."   In my opinion
the production of Jacobean
or Stuart work worthy of
such names is impossible

FIG. 80.

without the aid of the chisel, and we are therefore glad
to be able to place before our readers these carefully
executed designs, showing the correct thing to cut

FIG. 81.

when they are called upon to enrich work produced
under such nomenclature.

It will be noticed that there is much "flat" or surface carving in these examples, and they may be easily
traced.   Fig. 78 offers a fine example for the learner

to practice on. The lines are easily followed and little "rounding off" is required.

I give three more examples of surface carving in Fig. 81. These are Arabian carved panels, and are very fine. They are shown here rather as examples of what can be done, than to be followed.

We now close this chapter and will take up carving proper in the next.

CHAPTER V

ROUNDED FORMS OR CARVING PROPER

It will now be in order to take up work that is more difficult and more artistic than any we have yet dealt with, namely, rounded work and foliage.

Contour or rounding and modeling, of course, correspond to light and shade, but plain gouge and cavo-cutting is simple *sketching*. Any animal, or a human figure, a vase, flowers or vines may be thus carved, the only further condition being that the outlines shall be broad and bold. Great care should be exercised not to make too many lines, especially fine ones, and in all cases to avoid detail and make the design as simple as you can. When in thus outlining an animal you have clearly indicated, with as few lines as possible, what it is meant to be, you have done enough, as in all sketching the golden rule is to give as much representation with as little work as possible (Fig. 82).

It may be observed that familiar and extensive practice of the very easy gouge groove work and of simple flat or cavo-cutting in hollows, if carried out on a *large* scale, as for instance in wall and door patterns, gives the pupil far more energy and confidence and is more conducive to free-hand carving and the sweep cut than the usual method of devoting much time in the beginning to chipping elaborate leaves and other small work. Therefore it will be well for the pupil to perfect himself in such simple groove and hollow work. This was the first step in mediæval carving, and it was the proper one for general decoration. It was in this manner that the old carvers of England and their masters, the Flemings, taught their pupils.

Compared with plant forms, examples of which we will illustrate later on, the ˙elements drawn from the animal kingdom are few in number; this is very probably due to the greater difficulty experienced in adapting these forms for decorative purposes; it is

FIG. 82.

certainly not advisable to introduce the animal form too frequently. With some nations, too, religious difficulties stood in the way—the Mohammedan religion forbidding the representation of any living beings; and further, the restriction was applied to vegetable forms, too, and this has resulted in the art of the Mohammedan being based almost entirely upon geometrical principles.

It will be found that the same rules which guided the

selection of plant forms apply to the selection of animal forms, viz., (1) the ornamental possibilities of

FIG. 83.

the form, and (2) the symbolic nature of the forms. These decided what particular members of either kingdom should be used in decorative schemes principally,

Those animal forms most used in historic ornament are the lion, tiger and panther amongst the wild animals, and the horse, ox, dog and goat amongst the domesticated animals. The dolphin (Fig. 83) is the only generally used representative of ocean life; but it has been very largely used, partly because of its ornamental possibilities and partly because of its symbolic significance. Amongst birds the only form that has largely entered into decorative design has been the eagle. Other birds have been employed, but mostly in an auxiliary manner, chiefly naturalistic, as in the enriching of scroll ornament, in which birds, reptiles, insects, as well as built-up artificial forms, cherubs and similar elements, were used; but no other bird appears to have been used as a principal ornament typical of any artistic principle so much as the eagle.

Amongst animal forms we may class those mythical animals which are known as dragons and griffins (Fig. 84). Separate parts of animals, such as heads and wings, are used as independent elements. Lions' heads and the wings of doves, ducks, geese, as well as bats, are used in this connection. Wings are attached to mythical animal forms such as the dragon, also to angels and to imps. In providing angels and cherubs with wings, it may be remarked that doves' and pigeons' wings are most generally used; they are often conventionalized and extended, but this particular form of wing provided the general idea, whilst a bat's wing forms the basis for the use of wings for Satanic purposes.

Other forms—such as that of the serpent, because, principally, of its symbolic meaning and use, and the shell, because of its ornamental possibilities—have been largely used at different times. The lamb was

FIG. 84.

sometimes used in Christian ornament, generally in conjunction with the cross.

Grotesque heads of animals were used very largely in buildings of the Gothic period, in addition to grotesque human heads.

Human Figures.—The representation of the human form has, since man became sufficiently developed to accurately portray it, been a favorite element of decoration. It has been used in a very large measure as symbolical of seasons, hours and elements, as virtues and vices, good and evil, strength and grace, and many other attributes and qualities, both real and abstract. The gods have always been represented as "glorified men," and angels and devils have partaken of man's physical form.

The human form, too, has been represented very often solely on account of its decorative value: as being the highest possible expression of art and beauty.

There are some fine examples in existence in Europe and this country of chests and cabinets decorated with human figures principally in full relief; that is, the figures are complete in themselves.

This full use of the actual human figure is not, however, so common as the use of the conventionalized figure; generally, this takes the shape of portions of it, being used either separately or in conjunction with other arbitrary and conventionalized forms, such as occur in their use in satyrs, centaurs, Neptunes, mermaids and sphinxes, or as grotesque masks, the Medusa head, cherub heads, and cherubs and cupids, and it is sometimes used to represent Death, as in the skull and crossbones.

The use of the mask appears to have originated in

Greece, and to have been transferred for use in the theaters. As they were used in this connection to represent certain characters, the use of certain definite forms of masks became attached to certain definite characters, and gradually they became elements of decoration and were used to represent certain artistic principles. They were extensively used in the Renaissance period, sometimes in conjunction with other elements, as where the mask forms a center from which spring flowers and fruit, and as where the mask forms the terminal ornament of a scroll or stalk.

The mask was often employed in a grotesque form, often being treated entirely as a caricature, leaves being used as beard and hair, and other elements often being employed to represent certain portions of the face which the mask represented. These grotesque masks were largely used by the artists of the Middle Ages, both Gothic and Renaissance.

Enough has been said to indicate what the elements of decoration are, and we will now give some of the principles upon which these elements are built up into designs suitable for wood carving purposes.

Having got a clear idea as to what elements may be used, we are ready to build them together to form designs for our work. We may decide to use either geometrical forms, natural forms, .artificial forms, animals or the human figure, either separately or combined, and the combination may consist of any of the elements of decoration. Whatever we decide to use will be built up or put together to form the design according to the following principles:

1. Even distribution.
2. Order.
3. Balance.

4. Proportion.
5. Repetition.
6. Alteration.
7. Symmetry.
8. Radiation.
9. Variety.
10. Contrast.
11. Fitness.
12. Repose.

These are the main principles that govern the elaboration of design. It should also be noted that ornament should always be employed in such a manner as to emphasize the member it is used to decorate; it should never hide or destroy its outline and shape.

It should also be used with a definite regard for the outlines of the member; that is, the boundary or margin lines should contain the whole of the design. There are exceptions to this rule which will be taken into account at a later period, but it is as well to work from this rule at the first until sufficient progress has been made to warrant a departure from it.

Even Distribution.—This means that whatever space we have at our disposal should be filled by the elements we are using, duly observing a certain balance between the elements and the groundwork. Fig. 85 gives illustrations showing good and bad methods of distribution. In the sketch marked A it will be noticed that a balance exists between the groundwork and the design; there is not a big amount of space followed by a close gathering or congregation of elements. Notice, too, that the corners of the rectangle are well and evenly filled. Sometimes it occurs that a design is made for a rectangular shape that would better fill a shape having a domed top margin, as

shown in the sketch marked B by the dotted lines.   It
can without difficulty be seen where the uneven distribution lies.   The spaces marked X require filling;
but it should be remarked that judgment has to be
exercised in the filling; any element stuck in only for
the express purpose of filling up the space will not do.

It should be taken as a primary rule that all parts of
a design should be absolutely necessary in its building
up; all elements made use of should each fulfill a pur-

Fig. 85.

pose, having a definite reason for its use with regard
to the artistic necessities of the whole design, and not
merely because of its being required to "fill up."   And
further, in a complete and well thought out design
any element which may be taken away would mar the
construction and effect of the design.   A design
should be so well constructed that no portion can be
taken away without impoverishing its general conception and completeness.

It is possible to fill up any unnecessary open spaces

with elements that do not suggest that such was the intentional object in so using them, because the design may have, in its original conception, been deficient in just these elements and at just that particular point, so that their addition does not mar but actually completes the design. This does not often occur, however, and when it does the student may consider himself fortunate that such is the case. A design is at fault respecting even distribution when it is complete so far as the general conception and use of the elements are concerned, that is, when the addition or subtraction of another element would spoil its construction and effect, and it does not then conform to the law of even distribution; when, on the one hand, it is obvious that other elements are required to fill out the spaces and that this cannot be done without, on the other hand, destroying the constructive value of the design.

Order.—A consideration of this principle leads us to the conclusion that our designs should be well considered as to the relations and proportions that should exist between their various parts; and that a certain definite plan should be followed in the building up of the designs. Order should be observed both in the selection and in the distribution of the elements. This implies that a certain unity should exist between all the parts of a design.

All the elements should be selected with a view to their probable combination; and this combination of elements should be well and carefully considered with regard to the effect to be produced in connection with the object the design is for. Further reference will be made to "Order" in the next chapter.

Balance and Proportion.—These principles are of the very greatest importance. In the first place, in constructing any design it should be well considered as to the proportion that shall exist between the various parts of the article to be carved. It is a very common thing—much too common—to see the whole of the exposed surfaces of an article carved, and that, too often, in the most lavish manner and with not a plain relieving surface of any description; often enough, too, the defining edges of mouldings, which should mean so much to the whole effect of the conception, are rounded over or cut up by elements of the design, and thus their distinctive value is destroyed and the very reason for their existence is ignored. There are at least two good reasons why furniture should not be carved over its entire surface as a rule; one is that the effect of each separate design is in danger of being killed or destroyed by that of the adjoining designs, and the other is that it produces a sense of unrest and often irritation—the whole article gives you the impression of being too "busy," too much cut up; there is no place upon which the eye can rest to obtain relief from the effect of the carved work.

We do not say that objects should *never* be covered with carving, because attention need only be called to Indian and other Oriental carving to see that success can be gained by such treatment; but it needs a very great gift as a designer to so balance the various designs for the different members, and to so arrange them as regards proportion of mass and line, large and important elements with smaller and less important, and so forth, as to gain that repose that is necessary to all good design; and it does not appear that Western artists have been as successful in this respect as the Eastern ones.

We, generally, in thinking out any scheme of design have some particular panel or element or feature to which we wish to give a special interest, and which, therefore, requires to be so treated that more than ordinary attention shall be drawn to it; and it is this, it seems to me, that requires the use of plain mouldings or framework or other similar feature spoken of, to so give it the necessary emphasis.

With regard to the application of these principles of balance and proportion to the production of the actual design, the same remarks substantially apply.

Regard should be had to the proportion existing between the space to be ornamented and the elements used, especially bearing in mind the distance from the eye at which the ornamentation is to be placed eventually; this consideration should enter very largely into any scheme of decoration.

The relation that should exist between the size and importance of the elements used in the design should be well considered, so as to get a design that shall be well balanced in all its parts.

A well-balanced and proportionate design should be based upon natural laws, so that harmony of parts results.

Repetition and Alteration.—The two principles may be taken together; they have enough of what is common to both to enable them to be considered together, and there is sufficient difference between them to enable them to be easily distinguished. Repetition consists in the same element being used in a continuous manner upon those members whose shape demands such use. Instances of such a requirement occur upon mouldings, borders, narrow upright stiles, rails, cornices, dado rails, picture mouldings, and other places which will be noticed by the student when considering schemes of ornament.   It occurs the most often, and its use is the more simple and unmeaning elements, as geometrical forms and figures and natural objects.   Chip carving will readily suggest itself to the student as affording an extensive manifestation of the principle of repetition, in which the simplest of all unmeaning forms are joined together to produce the homogeneous effect intended.   As we use more developed forms—forms which have more meaning in

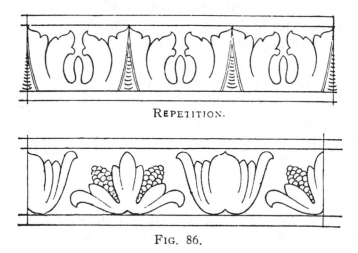

REPETITION.

FIG. 86.

themselves, either because of their artistic capabilities or from their symbolic meaning—we should use them with less frequency until, when we reach the last of the classes of elements, viz., the human figure, it should be used the least of any element in this connection.

A study of the elements employed in design and their use throughout the historical periods of art, gives us the key to the use of repetition and its place in decorative design.   It is that the less meaning, from the points of view of either beauty or symbolism, a form possesses, the more legitimate is its use as a repeated element; it not only does not offend our perceptions, but it appears to be absolutely necessary to gain the object aimed at.

But the more meaning an element expresses, the more should it be emphasized; and it can only be emphasized by being isolated, either by the absence of other decoration, by being surrounded by either plain ground, or the straight lines given by mouldings surrounding, or by less developed and more unmeaning elements.

And this means that the more beauty or symbolism shown by an element, the less frequently should it be employed. This question of the varying interest possessed by various elements, and how they should be arranged with regard to the wellbeing of the whole design, will be further considered under the head of Fitness.

Alteration is the alternate repetition of the same element, the intervals being filled with other elements.

This is sometimes done when it is considered necessary to use a certain element because of its symbolic nature, which makes it appropriate to the article to be decorated; but when such element being repeated without other elements it would induce monotony, or would have its full effect considerably modified by repetition, it is in such cases introduced at intervals only, the spaces between being filled by elements of a lesser interest.

Symmetry.—This principle is very closely having the leading lines upon which we build our elements, and which form the "skeleton" of the design, equal on both sides.

In most designs it does not necessarily follow that all the details of the design should be the same on both sides, although that would follow if we carried out this principle to its fullest extent. But the principle of Variety suggests that such is not necessary. If we apply it to the leading lines—the general appearance only—it will be carrying the application of the law quite as far as is necessary. This especially applies to designs whose extent is fairly large and in which the departure in detail from a symmetrical plan would not be injurious to the general proportion and

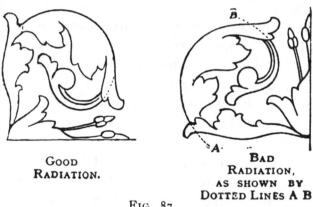

GOOD
RADIATION.

BAD
RADIATION,
AS SHOWN BY
DOTTED LINES A B

FIG. 87.

balance of the design, and where such departure would not be obtrusive in character. But it would be as well to remark that beginners will be well advised if they strictly adhere to the general rule of symmetry for a considerable time, at any rate until they have made such progress that their artistic sense and judgment have developed so far as to enable them to feel when and where and to what extent the law of Variety dictates or suggests a departure from the law of Symmetry. Let it be borne in mind that a very definite and cogent reason must always exist to render any departure from a general principle advisable. It should not be done for any fanciful reason; the reason should be *felt;* in fact, it should follow almost as a matter of course, from a consideration of the whole design and the elements used.

Radiation.—This law is a very essential feature in any system of decorative design. In most designs points exist from which the leading lines apparently proceed, and other subordinate points exist from which minor elements, such as buds and flowers, spring. These are the points of radiation.

Radiation is of three kinds:

(1) That which springs from a single point.

(2) That which springs from a vertical line.

(3) That which springs from a horizontal line.

An illustration of the first is a flower, such as the daisy, in which all the petals spring or radiate from the center. A well-formed anthemion illustrates the second kind of radiation, and an example of the third kind is afforded by a border consisting of a single leaf repeated, every leaf springing from or radiating from the lower line or margin of the border.

Many otherwise good designs are quite ruined by a disregard of this vital principle. All good design should have its elements radiating perfectly, in a good curve, and with just that kind of curve which most nearly fulfills the requirements demanded by Proportion and Balance to make this curve natural, easy and yet strong. Just what curve will meet these requirements the student must find out by constant study, observation and practice; by giving a certain definite amount of time each day to drawing, the knowledge of the conditions attending good radiation will gradually unfold itself to the student.

It is, it may be remarked, not necessary to continue the elements quite up to the point of radiation; a considerable distance may separate them, but it should be well understood that the element should have its appearing point so placed with relation to its general direction and the curves of its outlines that it suggests quite readily its source and origin; and if it is joined by a light pencil line to its source, the line so produced should be in exact correspondence with what we should expect to be the case if the principle of radiation is observed—that is, it should be of a good curve and direction, without any lameness or break in its contour; it should be strong and vigorous, and the relation between the curve and the weight and extent of ornament it has to bear should be kept well in mind.

Variety and Contrast.—Variety has been called "the salt of ornament that cures the insipidity of repetition." Monotony often results from the continued repetition of any element; but if variety is introduced judiciously, with good taste, and with a sense of the fitness of things, this monotony need never appear.

Variety can be introduced in so many different ways that each stage of designing can afford to the student an interest it would not otherwise possess.

In building or planning the design it can be kept in view by the arrangement of the leading lines, by choosing the various elements to be used and by arranging them so that the necessary contrast is obtained; and in the arrangement of the details variety can be brought in by the use of different elements in similar corresponding places so as to avoid that monotony that is often induced by the too regular occurrence of the same element. The treatment it is proposed to give to the elements should also be kept in mind; this has much to do in deciding what particular element should be used in a given place. It is not always the *size* of the element that is the important point, but its *surface*, whether smooth or broken up.

Variety depends very largely upon the elements available for its full use. From age to age these have varied, and the art of each period has gained or suffered by the profusion or poverty that existed at that particular time. It reached its highest point in the late Renaissance, when natural and artificial foliage, artificial objects, animals and the human figure were very extravagantly employed. In chip carving, perhaps, our use of elements is most strictly confined. Few elements are used, and repetition has necessarily to be very largely employed. In introducing variety it should be the aim of the student to do so only when, as already pointed out, a distinct necessity for such use arises. If this is not kept well in view, a tendency will arise and rapidly develop to introduce it in a very lavish manner, and the result of this would be that other principles would be utterly disregarded and the design ruined. Exercise restraint in using your material and remember that the success of the design does not depend upon using one principle excessively to the disregard of the others, and that success is much more likely to be gained by a due consideration of *all* the principles of design and of *all* the requirements of the article to be ornamented.

Fitness.—Under this head comes the consideration of the material, the kind and quantity of the elements and their subsequent arrangement and the style of article to be decorated.

It will easily be understood by woodworkers in

general that certain kinds of wood lend themselves naturally to designs consisting of big, strong, "lumpy" elements. Oak, ash and pine are examples; the grain is wide and unsuitable for fine work involving the introduction of small elements. Oak can be obtained of fine, close grain; but generally speaking, broad effects are more suitable to it and more easily obtained in it than, *e.g.*, sycamore.

Other woods, as, *e.g.*, boxwood and ebony, are, because of their size and texture, only suited to finer work, and the designs suitable for working in either of these woods should be fitted to their peculiarities of grain. In like manner, all woods differ in their ability to give the best expression to any particular design, and this should be well considered by the student in evolving his designs. Wood also is weak in a direction "across the grain," and any design made should be influenced by this consideration. With regard to the kind and quantity of the elements, the selection of these should be governed by the demands of the article to be carved and the particular parts or members to be ornamented.

And this applies also to the arrangement or general plan employed in their building up. By a judicious selection of elements and a well-judged and carefully thought out plan, the design can be made to suit the article so that the necessary emphasis is given to those parts that need such attention being called to them.

Repose.—This is often sadly absent from designs. So many are the elements introduced, and so little care is exercised in their arrangement, that the effect obtained is one of irritation; the whole design seems worried to death by an attempt to give richness and variety. Too much contrast is fatal to the wellbeing of the design. Simplicity, not richness, should exercise the most influence with the student. Repose is induced by

(1) A suitable arrangement of the elements;

(2) A suitable method of treatment.

The latter is a very powerful agent in getting that repose necessary.

The surface should not be cut up and scored across by means of many gouge cuts, without there being a corresponding amount of plain surface introduced in such manner that it balances the many gouge cuts.

Plain, smooth surfaces have a very great value as decorative agents, and should be plentifully introduced.

We are now, having obtained some knowledge of what elements are used in design and the principles upon which they are arranged, in a position to build up any design by using or arranging the elements in accordance with the principles given.

The spaces and sizes of spaces to which design can be applied are so varied and numerous that it is impossible, in a short series, to give examples illustrating each and every shape possible. There is the parallelogram, circle, ellipse, triangle, spandrel, column, pilaster, octagon, hexagon and many other shapes both of regular and irregular forms.

Varied though these forms and shapes are, however, there is a similarity as regard their planning; there is a certain principal course to adopt that is the same throughout, varying only in the modification necessary to adapt the general plan of the design to the necessities of the shape.

This being so, we cannot do better than select the parallelogram as the object of our present work, and we will show how a design, or designs, should be built up by the application of the principles described to a rectangular shape, such as a square or an oblong, these forms being easy of application as panels or pilasters, bosses, etc.

It should, in the first place, be decided just what particular kind of carving it is intended to adopt in the scheme of decoration, because this has much to do in deciding just how to build the design and what elements to use in its composition.

If it is intended to execute the work in very high relief, then the principal consideration should be that of "mass."

The object of high relief work is to produce deep, black shadows, which, when contrasted with the light reflected from the raised portions, produce a definite effect in light and shade; and when the shadows are well arranged, so that a good balance and a certain specific proportion exist between them, then the work may be considered good. It may be remarked here that high relief should be decided upon from a consideration of the above principles of balance and proportion of light and shade. I am afraid it is often introduced from a desire to "show off"—the desire to show an admiring world how clever the artist is, both in the design and execution. This is always bad and should be avoided as you would avoid poison. In all periods the degenerate in art has been and can be identified by this tendency, and the result is extravagance of ornament, both in conception and execution, without any connection with, or consideration of, its real decorative value.

In low relief work, on the other hand, the chief consideration is that of "line"; that is to say, the decorative value of the design depends upon the arrangement

of the curves and principal lines.   There is no attempt
to produce deep, black shadows; the whole effect is
produced by beauty of curve and the particular arrangement of the outlines of the design.

Between these extremes lie many gradations, each
combining more or less the two principles of mass and
line.   Most designs for ordinary amateur's work, or,
for that matter, any work, are built up upon a consideration of both principles.

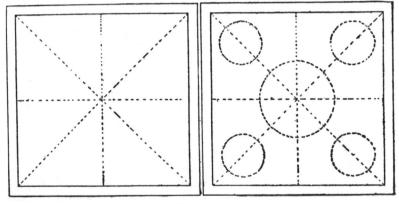

Fig. 87½.

The question will arise, naturally, as to what it is
that governs the use of either principle.   Broadly
speaking, high relief should be used in any place
where it is obvious some ornament should be, but that
is too far removed from the eye to enable any detail
work to be seen or appreciated.   It is in just such a
position as this that the broad effects of light and
shade produced by this method are most valuable.

Low relief can be used, and is the most suitable, in
places nearer to the eye, where the effect produced by
the beautiful curves, the close detail and the delicate
cutting can be most appreciated.

It can be seen that if high relief is desired, then the design will be built up upon the arrangement of mass. The position of the masses will be decided upon first; then they will be joined by stalks or bands, etc., as may be determined, and the character to be assumed by the masses decided upon—that is, as to whether they will be flowers, fruit or foliage, animals or birds, or human figures. In Figs. 87½ and 88 is shown a square panel, and in the sketches comprising the series

FIG. 88.

are shown the various steps leading from an entirely blank surface to the completed design.

In the first place we determine the position and general arrangement of the masses, which in this case consist of a central large mass surrounded by four smaller masses.

The next step consists in joining the masses in a decorative yet intelligent and natural manner. In order to do this we must decide just what form and character the masses are to partake of. It will be obvious that the central mass should be of the greater interest, since its position and size render it capable of being invested with greater significance. This be ng so, we can decide to make the central mass into a head, either that of an animal, or, if we are very ambitious, we could decide upon a human head. We will, however, not go quite so far as this just at present, and will content ourselves with a mask. The four other minor masses may be determined into flowers. It will then be apparent how we can connect the various masses together in a natural and decorative manner, by causing the flowers to spring from the central mass by means of stalks. These can be flanked by leaves, or can have any suspicion of stiffness modified or counterbalanced by the introduction of ribbon work or strap work.

In deciding what details should be used in the composition of the masses, the distance of the panel from the eye should always be kept in mind; if this be effectually done, the mistake of putting in too much detail will be avoided. In this connection it may be as well to call the attention of students to the peculiar ornament called the "mask," used by the stone carvers of the thirteenth century, sometimes as a hood mould; sometimes also it is found in corbel-tables. Seen at a small distance, this appears to be merely a peculiarly shaped terminal, but when placed in its proper position, at least several feet from the eye, it assumes the appearance of a human face, somewhat grotesque, no doubt, but nevertheless reproducing faithfully the lights and shadows that go towards the composition of the face of a strongly marked individuality, as in Fig. 88. If this panel has been well designed, it should answer to the tests which may be applied by means of our knowledge of the principles described and set forth previously. It should, for instance, be well and evenly distributed as regards the elements; it should be symmetrical, so far as the masses are concerned, although these masses may be differently treated in respect of their detail, *e.g.*, one of the four minor masses may be a full flower, another a bud, and so forth, always having a regard to their balance and proportion. Likewise, these principles of balance and proportion should be taken into account in the arrangement of the strap work and ribbon work, etc., so that all the minor parts should help to *emphasize* the more important members, rather than detract from their true appearance and effect as masses.

All minor parts should be subordinate in character (and this should be remembered in their treatment), and should never be given such importance as will cause them to obtrude themselves upon our notice to the detriment of the more important members.

In such systematic manner should these principles be applied to the finished design, until the student unconsciously begins to use them in the production of his designs, until he has made their consideration a part of his artistic self.

I should like at this stage to point out the great importance of the due consideration of the principle of restraint. When we have reached a certain stage in our artistic evolution we feel ourselves apparently capable of designing anything, even of reaching to the heights attained by Grinling Gibbons, Michael Angelo, or Niccola Pisano, and as a consequence we rush into the commitment of the most absurd extravagances. This is, no doubt, very interesting to the sociologist, as showing how clearly and automatically even we reflect in our actions our inner impulses; but it is quite fatal to our ambitions to produce sound design that will last through the succeeding centuries, as the works of the above-mentioned artists have remained through the intervening periods, and are still with us, undiminished in their excellence, undimmed in their glory by the centuries that have passed.

A *résumé* of this article shows us that design should be built up as follows:

(1) If in high relief, it should be arranged according to mass.

(2) The elements to be used should be decided upon, having due regard to their suitability for the purpose intended.

(3) Plan the masses with due regard to proportion, balance, symmetry, etc.

(4) Connect them by suitable elements into a unified whole, applying the principle of subordination to the minor and connecting elements.

(5) Fill in the details of the masses, having due regard to the distance of the panel from the eye, and the manner in which the carving will ultimately be lighted.

We have here attempted, in a brief and concise manner, to show how design is begun and to show in as accurate a manner as possible how it is ultimately built up. It would be as well for the student to now practice upon these lines. Take a square and try to arrange it in *some other way* than that above described. And it would be as well here to mention what may be termed "the personal element." This differs with each one, and is the cause of the wide difference that exists between our individual work. This personal element is not made by, and is very little under the control of, the principles spoken of in the last chapter. It should be allowed to have comparatively free play, so that the work produced by each student may be stamped with that originality and individuality which are very much lacking at the present time.

The student should now have advanced far enough, providing practice has been obtained, to do some more important work than we have hitherto undertaken. It should be remembered and well borne in mind continually that it is not sufficient, by any means, to *know how to do* the work; it is very necessary to have sufficient manual skill *to be able to do it;* and this can only come by means of incessant practice. Without wishing to discourage any student, it may be stated that it is the opinion of the writer that perfect control of the tools is obtainable only by years of practice.

The object of this lesson is to introduce a design which presents greater difficulties than we have yet encountered. This design, Fig. 89, possesses various points of interest, although many of the elements used in its composition will be familiar to those who have closely followed this course. The particular points of interest to which I wish to call special attention are (1) the berries, and (2) the use of perspective.

The first-named are apt to be a stumbling-block to many; in fact, to most beginners there is always a difficulty in getting the berries proportionate with one another, and as regards the general mass, and in getting them a good "fat" shape, so that they may play their full part in providing that amount of broken surface essential to the wellbeing of the design.

In this design berries occur only in two places, but they are sufficient for our purpose.

It should be noted that this class of ornament should be sparingly used, as a rule. The object of including berries in a design is, not to show the berries themselves, or to give utterance to the skill of the carver, but to provide that amount of regular and organized broken surface that the necessities of good design demand.

This is a principle too often overlooked. The

FIG. 89.

designer should have in view the value of his scheme of design, looked at from the standpoint of decorative design; its value as a scheme of decorative design looked at *as a whole* should be more important to him than the insertion of certain flowers, fruit or foliage as being elements that possess *in themselves* a certain beauty or decorative value.

The disregard of this principle often results in a too great abundance of this class of element, because of the "effect" it produces; notably in cheap furniture, upon which readers have probably often seen V cuts or flutings crossing each other to produce either an imitation of Chippendale tracery or an appearance of berries.

FIG. 90.

With regard to the actual work in this panel, which is that of a clock door, readers who have followed the previous lessons will have little difficulty in preparing the groundwork, by first taking the V tool and cutting a trench around the design to protect the corners and other delicate parts, then setting in and taking out the superfluous wood. The ground should be about $\frac{3}{16}$ to ¼ inch depth, and it should be quite smooth and uniform; in the photo of this design the ground, it will be noticed, is punched, but this is not necessary, and it should be the aim of the students to get the ground well enough done to dispense with this artificial aid to effect.

In "setting in" around the berries, it is better to proceed as in Fig. 91, "setting in" along the lines *a a;* this protects the berries from damage to their outlines when taking out the ground. It should, however, be

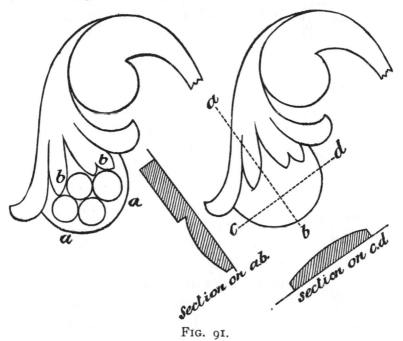

FIG. 91.

pointed out that the tools should not be driven in too far, else the cuts made by them show upon the ground when we have cut the berries back to their ultimate outline. Now cut the berries back; this can easily be done now, and this treatment ensures a firm and clean edge to their outline.

The next step in carving the berries is rather important; beginners generally "set in" each separate berry now, and the result is that the whole mass of berries presents a *flat*, uniform and monotonous appearance

The better way is to "set in" along the edge of the calyx, marked *b b* in Fig. 91, and then model the surface of the berries as in Fig. 91, treating them as one whole mass and giving it a section as in Fig. 91.

spade tool

FIG. 92.

In this way the whole mass of the berries partakes of the general shape of the member or element they spring from, and it effectually prevents them being all in the same plane and thereby inducing monotony. Of course, it will be noticed that the pencil lines have gone, and we can now redraw them, or merely allow the tool to outline them; the latter is better training for the eye. In this connection it is maintained by some carvers that every one who aspires to be a credit to the profession should be able to dispense with pencil lines; especially is this the case with solid work where the original pencil lines, if ever there, have all been cut away. This may seem to be too severe, and in many cases quite unnecessary; but it has this great virtue, that if it is set before the student as an ideal at which to aim, he unconsciously strengthens his sense of proportion, accuracy of judgment of distance and curve.

It may be pointed out here that the size of the berries is an important consideration. They should be proportionate to the size of the member they adjoin or spring from, and they should never be *too small;* keep them on the large side; if too small they appear to be too insignificant and lose thereby in true effect.

The next step is to outline them with whatever tool most nearly fits the curve; a "spade tool" is the best to use for modeling berries, Fig. 92; the particular shape of these tools enables them to be worked into corners an ordinary tool will not touch. The result will appear as in Fig. 93.

Where the cuts join one another will appear triangular spaces; these will be taken out and a small platform will be left; the spade tool by being tilted will sink these triangular platforms until all the cuts meet at a point. It is needless to say that clean, accurate cutting is necessary, and the tool points or corners need to be quite sharp and pointed. It will be found of advantage sometimes to have tools ground for left and right hand to better enable

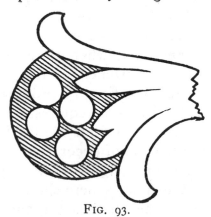

FIG. 93.

the berries to be cut clean down to the lowest point.

The tool used to clean off the surface of the berries should be as near the curve of the surface as it is possible to be, so that the berries will be free from unnecessary tool marks. It is sometimes thought necessary to finally take a gouge, the exact curve of the outline of the berries, and lightly "set in" around the outline by hand; this gives a definiteness to the berries which they often lack.

A common fault is to get the berries flat, too much being taken off the sides, leaving the berries *pointed* at the end and with distinct *ridges* down the sides where the two marks meet.   This can partially be avoided by holding the gouge quite horizontal when beginning the cut for rounding the berries, and then taking it *slowly* over.   Do not have the berries all one size; this especially refers to large clusters; it is evident that the berries in the center should be the largest, those at the sides being the smaller, because of the demand of perspective.

This law or principle of perspective is in the flowers in this particular design, and will now be considered. When flowers are shown quite full face, each petal is practically the same size, and it is treated in a similar manner; but when they are *tilted*, some of the petals are foreshortened; in fact, they all are affected by the altered position, in proportion to the amount of tilt, and each petal requires somewhat different individual treatment to make it play its full and effective part in the scheme of decoration.

As the design is sunk only ¼ inch, it is obvious that as the flowers here shown are, roughly speaking, 1½ or 2 inches in diameter, and they are tilted, they would have a portion of their width and depth lying *behind* the plane of the ground as shown in Fig. 94, this being a longitudinal section of that part of the panel; and, similarly, the front petal and part of the side petals would be projecting in front of the surface of the panel. This, of course, is an impossible way of treating the flowers, and so we arrange them so that it appears as if the flower had been pressed up against the background and has its back or top petal forced forward and the front petal made to lie backwards and downwards, as at *b*, Fig. 94.

In this position we must make it appear that the

flower is tilted at an angle intended by the designer; and it must be said that a great deal depends upon the manner of treatment adopted.

It will be noticed in the photograph that the back petals are *hollowed*, as per Fig. 95, *a*, whilst the front petals are made *full* and *round*, as at *b*, Fig. 95. The side petals should be carved as at *c*, Fig. 95; these sections, it should be borne in mind, are cross sections at right angles to the direction of the petals. With regard to the centerpiece representing the stamens, etc., this should be inclined at a suitable angle to the plane of the ground. In the photo it is shown rounded; an alternative is to hollow it, and then sink a cut in it, as shown at *c*, Fig. 95. This apparently throws the center farther back and completes the illusion, if it may be so termed, of depth.

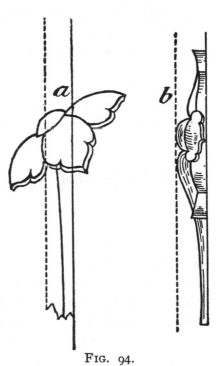

FIG. 94.

Sometimes the center portion of the flower is sunk below the level of the ground, especially when the ground is taken out only ⅛ inch or less; this is quite legitimate, but should be rather sparingly adopted; it has the best effect when only occasionally used.

It may be remarked that a common error into which beginners often fall is to overdo certain aids to effect,

As in the case here illustrated, they are so struck by the effect produced by a simple "trick" (it may be truly so called) like this that they at once apply it to every flower upon their work, and thereby assist in the failure of their work as a scheme of decoration.

An occasional element treated in the manner described may be conducive to the *general good*, but a whole series of elements so treated would be very much open to question.

Most of the difficulties which are likely to be

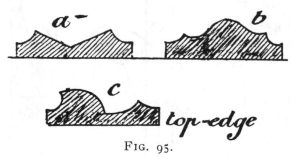

FIG. 95.

encountered by the beginner have now been mentioned and explained, and the student should be ready for a really difficult piece of work. This is provided by the panel, the design for which is given in Fig. 96.

One or two new elements are introduced, · the principal being the dragon in the center. This winged dragon is really the chief object of interest in the panel, the other elements merely constituting a "setting" for it; consequently it should receive a special amount of care and attention.

It will also be noticed that the groundwork is not punched and that it has no margin, but the ground is taken quite to the edge of the panel. This latter fact makes the carving stand out further than it would if it possessed a margin, and this enhances the effect. In working the panel, proceed as in previous examples. Trace the design from center or margin lines (center lines preferred) to ensure it being on the wood true and square, then run the V tool round the elements to relieve the pressure of the surrounding wood, then "set in" and proceed to take out the ground. The ground should be sunk to a depth of not more than $\frac{5}{16}$ inch; $\frac{1}{4}$ inch is sufficient, although beginners would naturally imagine that a design containing an element of the nature of the dragon, with its wide body and various prominent peculiarities, should stand quite a

FIG. 96.

long way off the ground. Reference will be made to this later.

The size of the panel, which should be in hard wood (oak or walnut preferably), is 30 inches by 12 inches and should be $\frac{5}{8}$ inch or $\frac{3}{4}$ inch in thickness. Gauge the depth ($\frac{1}{4}$ inch) around the edge of the board with either a single prick gauge or a pencil, and proceed to ground out as already described.

Get the ground uniformly level and as smooth as possible; and it may be here remarked that a ground finished off with the carving tool and showing the marks of the tool is of more value than a ground leveled down with the "router" and taken absolutely level and smooth.   It has a greater educational value, because of the really genuine ability it implies, and it also, in our opinion, has a *greater decorative value* because of the tool marks and the clean, crisp way in which they are cut.

Take care that in the grounding, or rather in the preliminary "wasting away" of the wood, the quick gouge is not taken too deeply, or the cuts will show afterwards.   It will be noticed in the panel illustrated that this has occurred at the top about a foot from the right-hand end.   Make all cuts meet each other, and

FIG. 97.

always cut with the grain where possible; and where it is necessary to cut against the grain use the sweep cut before described.   In this way the carving partakes of that shiny character of surface that has in itself the greatest decorative value, and stamps the work as being that of a carver who possesses more than an elementary knowledge of the grain of wood and the treatment that is due to it.   Many a fine piece of wood has been mutilated and utterly spoiled in the most fearful manner by being hacked and torn with just as fearfully blunt tools against the grain and across it, and in any way but the right way.

All these remarks apply particularly to modeling. Let the tool be perfectly sharp, so that it can have a chance to show what it *can* do; don't be afraid to use the strop from time to time, and whenever a tool shows the least sign of dullness or has the tiniest "gap" in it, attend to it at once.

All cuts, especially the finishing cuts, should be clean, smooth and crisp. In modeling this design, it may be as well for the student to turn and read again the remarks given on the necessity for a due arrangement of mass, how some parts, the least important, should be subordinated to others, the most important; some parts should be sunk to the ground or thereabouts, while others should be kept raised the full height. In so arranging the masses, always do so from the collective standpoint of the welfare of the whole design, so that all the parts shall be in harmony and that one part shall not be given unduly prominent effect at the obvious expense of another equally important part. One tendency observable in the evolution of the beginner is that of wishing to give undue prominence to one particular portion of the carving because of its great beauty, irrespective of any possibility of thereby destroying the harmony of the whole by so doing. Exercise restraint in treating any design, but especially do so when treating a design that has any element or elements that border upon the ornate and extravagant.

In this design the stalks can be kept low, swelling out in height as they swell out in width; the flower and the scroll at the right-hand end, the flower with the berries or seeds, and the one large leaf on the left end of the panel may be left full height; the other members lowered to whatever depth may seem best to the student, always keeping in mind the unity and harmony of the whole design. With regard to the treatment of the individual members themselves, after they have been taken to their respective levels, the law of variety, as applied to length and breadth and surface, should be applied. Sink one side of a leaf, as, *e.g.*, the leaf at the left lower corner of the design. This leaf is lowered at its top edge and kept raised at its lower edge, as a leaf, turning in the manner it does, naturally would appear. Other leaves should be twisted by being lowered at opposite corners before the surface by the ultimate and finishing cuts that give the leaf its final shape.

All cuts should have a definite relationship to the *curve* of the member or group of members, so that it emphasizes the curves. A careless cut, here and there, can very easily entirely spoil the character of the member; and often by so doing to one member can spoil the effect of the whole carving.

Notice in this panel how the ridges enable the eye to follow the curve; how the tool marks even act in a similar manner; how they all lead the eye in the direction the designer intended they should lead it; how beginning at the sources of the elements the eye is easily carried to the most ultimate point of each leaf and flower; and how, *vice versa*, beginning at the points or endings of the members, the eye is carried easily and obviously to the source of them all without break, without distraction, and therefore without annoyance. It is being able to do this that gives pleasure, that makes one feel that all the possibilities of the design have been realized, that the carver's powers of execution have been equal to his powers of conception.

In carving the berries, follow the instructions given,

and give special attention to the *outline* of the berries and the crevices between them.

With regard to the dragon, the photograph, Fig. 97, shows the method of treatment. It is, of course, quite an imaginative creation. No "dragon" as depicted in this design was ever in existence, but although imaginative in its present form, it is really based upon a combination of natural animal forms.

The griffin, an imaginative creature in use as an element of design from the earliest times, is the chief representative of this kind of ornament. It is a combination of the lion and the eagle, having a lion's body and the head and wings of the eagle. Sometimes we find the fore part of the griffin possessed of an eagle's legs and feet, the hind quarters being those of the lion. As men, in their eternal search after the new and strange, the novel and the original, became tired of existing elements and were limited in choice of entirely new objects (either natural or artificial) from which to draw new inspiration, they turned their attention to existing elements, and by a process of pulling to pieces and subsequent building up they produced the wonderfully varied grotesque forms found in Pompeian and Roman ornament; and subsequently in the Renaissance these forms were appropriated and developed. The present dragon possesses a head that might be a development of *either* an eagle or a lion; an eagle's wings, no feet or legs, and a fish's tail. The body is scaled, the scales extending each in the form of an entire ring around the neck and body. These scales may be cut up into smaller scales, as in Fig. 96, if thought necessary. It will be observed that the artificial leaf, which has been a feature of the designs used in this series, enters largely into the composition of the dragon. Its breast is covered with these leaves, springing from a line that is coincident with the outline of the bird; they form its beard, also its ears, and their influence is observable in the treatment of the tail. With reference to the wings, it will be observed that naturalness, grace and lightness characterize both their conception and treatment. Often these wings are too "wooden" and stiff, unnatural and ungraceful in both respects. Keep the feathers of varying lengths and widths, although it may be pointed out that this should not be overdone—there is a happy mean that should be sought for.

The use of tool marks is evident here; if the separate feathers are cleaned off quite smoothly, all the edges cut neatly and so on, then it will be evident that the workman who carved the wing was able to cut well and accurately; but it will not be evident that the wing has any suspicion of life beyond that suggested by its particular shape.

Something more than brilliant and accurate cutting is necessary; that inner perception of the true aim of the designer, which alone enables the worker to give a worthy interpretation of the design, is essential to all good work; and this inner perception can be gained by deep thought and study, by trying to fathom the meaning of the great works handed down to us from early times, and which are preserved in our museums and art galleries; and works, too, of recent years should be studied, so that by a process of comparison the student can learn the lessons to be drawn from these works.

The foregoing instructions app.y to the treatment of this design if sunk only to the depth of $\frac{1}{4}$ inch. But if it is desired to use the panel in a position that is a good distance from the eye, then the depth could be much greater, so that the consideration of mass, which is essential in such a case, shall receive the proper emphasis.

In this event, the principal attention should be given to the proportion of the masses, rather than to detail; in fact, too much attention to detail is quite unnecessary and would simply be labor thrown away.

At a distance all that is perceived of the design is mass and curve. Get the masses in proper proportion, so that a good balance exists between all parts, and pay attention to the cutting of the curves, and the design will be a success. Get this well grasped first, and let the details alone. The treatment of the individual parts will be as before described, but the differences in height and depth will be magnified. The cutting should be clean, strong and bold.

We now come to the consideration of the building up of a design, which is based upon the principle of "line." Perhaps it would be as well to point out that it is, in reality, almost impossible to separate mass from line. In nearly all really satisfactory designs both have to be considered to a greater or less extent. But it is evident that in originating any design it is attacked from either one or the other point of view— that of mass or line—and it should be well evident in the completed design from which point of view the artist started. If from that of mass, then the consideration of line has been, and should easily be seen to be, an auxiliary, a subordinate consideration. If from the point of view of lines, the opposite, of course, is the case. Surface carvings and all carvings in low relief should be considered from this point of view, that of "line." All these carvings are to be used in such a position that they are always comparatively close to the eye, and therefore details can be easily seen and appreciated —details such as clearness and sharpness of outline, beauty of curve, arrangement of small fruit, flowers and buds. It is not necessary to have any great effect of light and shade, as in the case of designs regulated by mass. Continuity and beauty of line and curve are the principal consideration.

It will then be evident that the designer should arrange the direction and distribution of the lines in the first place. If any mass is introduced afterwards, its size and position and character will be determined,

-SHOWING THE FORMATION OF A DESIGN.

FIG. 98.

necessarily, by the general arrangement of the lines of the design. In this case they will be subordinate to the "line" idea, as the latter was subordinate to the idea of mass in our first example, described in the last chapter.

The space at our disposal, then, is planned out by the use of what may be termed "leading" or principal lines. These lines determine the whole character of the design. They may be always visible, or may be quite obliterated by being covered with ornament; but they are always obvious, and form, as it were, the skeleton of the design. It is, therefore, of very great

importance that the "leading" lines should be planned
and arranged with great judgment and care; judicious
and careful thought should be expended upon their
arrangement, so that the ultimate design built upon
them shall be strong, vigorous and graceful. Figs. 98

No. 1   No. 2.

No. 3.   No 4.

Fig. 99.

and 99 give a series of illustrations showing the method
of filling in and arranging the "leading" lines. It will
be evident that their arrangement depends upon the
ultimate position of the panel; as to whether they
shall proceed from the side, or a corner, or an end, or

the middle; also, whether they shall partake of a radiating nature, or a horizontal, or a vertical position; and, of course, much depends upon the style we choose from which to take our elements and our inspiration. It can be said that designing from a consideration of "line" limits us more as regards the arrangement of the elements than designing from a consideration of "mass." We do not know what will be the size, or shape, or character of our masses until we have arranged the "leading" lines.

In practice it will be found, as has already been suggested, that unless we confine ourselves to designs of the nature of Celtic, in which the *motif* is entirely that of line, it will be impossible to arrange our leading lines without some consideration, however vague, of mass. Our modern designs are based very largely upon natural forms, and in nature the two ideas of "mass" and "line" are always found together; any design, therefore, which is true to nature should take into account both ideas. It should, however, be evident, as we have already said, from which position the design was conceived and thought out. Therefore, although we must consider to some extent what masses we intend using—their size and character—the design in this case must be approached from the point of view of arrangement of leading lines.

In planning the panel, its ultimate position will decide the character of the planning. We will consider that it is to be used as an independent panel, that is, it does not share with other panels or members in the entire scheme, but *is* the entire scheme in itself. We can then treat it in various ways. In the first place, we can arrange the leading lines over the whole of the space without reference to any center line or lines, as shown in the first set of sketches in Fig. 98.

In this case, care should be exercised in arranging the lines, because of the absence of an obviously symmetrical arrangement, and the tendency which naturally would follow this of falling into an arrangement that is deficient in order, and the difficulty of getting the design well balanced and well proportioned. It may be noted that designs built upon this arrangement are more suited to schemes which necessitate the panels being pairs, and in which, therefore, an equal balance can be maintained more naturally and easily. This arrangement can be used as a *single* panel, without another

FIG. 100.

with the same design reversed, when it is, for example, used as an end door of a sideboard, as in sketch, Fig. 100. In this case the drawers help, in a partial manner, to form the necessary balance required; it is more suitable used in this way than as a single panel forming a complete scheme. Take precautions to ensure the proper filling out of the corners in accordance with the principle of even distribution. It will be noticed throughout these sketches that both mass and line have been considered in planning; but it will also be noticed that line has been the chief consideration, and is well evident even in the finished sketch.

In the second set of sketches, Fig. 99, the arrangement is that of a design built upon two central lines, one horizontal, one vertical; in this, as is obvious, the whole of the design is contained in one quarter, being repeated and reversed to make the full design.

Although this arrangement may appear to be comparatively easy, because of the smaller space, and consequently fewer elements and a corresponding simplicity of plan, yet it is, perhaps, more difficult than the two preceding methods; at any rate, it is more difficult than the third method. This is so because of the fact that in arranging and considering only a quarter of the design, the appearance of the plan as a whole is not at once apparent; and it sometimes happens that what appeared to be suitable in the quarter design, is ill-balanced and badly arranged when the quarters are joined into the complete whole. It is, therefore, a better plan to consider the whole space rather than a quarter of it, and fill in, roughly perhaps, the leading lines in all four portions. This method will at least ensure their symmetrical and proportionate arrangement, and this is the principal consideration; the details can be filled in pretty easily.

Let me here emphasize the necessity of building designs upon a certain definite, organized plan; a plan which is strong, without being clumsy; vigorous without being ungraceful. To do this think out the leading lines with care; take time to consider their arrangement; do not unduly hurry that part of the process, and spend all the time in filling in detail work; a good, well arranged set of leading lines is much more important than the most exquisite detail that could be introduced.

It should be particularly noted that the student must familiarize himself with the leading principles treated of in previous parts, especially those of Even Distribution, Order and Symmetry. The consideration of these is especially applicable to the arranging of the leading lines.

When these are satisfactorily planned, and the masses suitably placed and decided upon, the detail can be filled in and its general disposal arranged.

For although we put in the leading lines first, yet we have had some idea as to what the detail would be like, and as to where it should be placed, and how; as, for instance, some of the lines we have intended to indicate the ultimate position of stalks, other lines the place of foliage and so forth. A certain general idea should be conceived as to what the full design should be before it is planned on paper. If this is not so, the design will in all probability be purely mechanical. It must be pointed out that all arrangements described in articles as to how to make designs, and all methods formulated, are aids only; the student must develop his own powers of conception by observation, practice and experiments; these rules and principles here laid down and described are for his *guidance* only; they show the manner of any experiment, the way to practice, and to mould his conceptions, so that they may be in accordance with the governing principles of design, and thereby express them in the best manner.

The mode of procedure with regard to the arrangement of "line" designs, is somewhat similar to that of "mass." It can be summed up as follows:

1. Decide upon the style and the elements to be adopted and used, having regard to the requirements of the space to be ornamented.

2. Decide upon the general arrangement of the design, such as whether it is to be a whole design or arranged upon a central line or lines.

3. Plan the space by means of leading lines, arranged upon a symmetrical and proportionate basis, and arrange what masses are to be used.

4. Build upon these leading lines the foliage and fruit or other elements decided upon. These lines may be entirely covered, but their existence will be evident, and should be, to save the design from appearing to be built upon an unarranged and indefinite plan.

Here we offer various designs the intention of which is to show how the principles of design may be applied. It may be said at once that there is no rigid, unalterable rule about the application of these principles. If that were so, all designs would bear a certain similarity that would indicate lack of originality. Originality or freshness of conception is only kept alive by interpreting the meaning and message of the elements from a separate individual standpoint. To do this successfully, we must not be bound too much by hard and fast rules.

It must be understood, then, that whilst the observance of these principles is essential to the production of good design, yet in their observance sufficient latitude is allowed for any number of designers to place their separate interpretation upon the elements and their arrangements to ensure designs that are quite different in meaning, character and treatment, although based upon the same *motif* and governed by the same principles.

A few words as to the choice of elements may be given here. As we have seen in previous pages, the elements are grouped under six heads; and as under each head we can find many varying forms, it would seem a rather difficult task to exercise a choice that would prove satisfactory. Personally, I have always found artificial foliage and forms to be the easiest elements to use in forming designs; there is a directness about them, an appearance that suggests the "manufactured article," that makes them easier to put into shape for wood carving purposes than using purely natural forms. The explanation is that these artificial forms have undergone a process of conventionalization at the hands of other artists, and have been handed down to us quite ready for immediate use. But this is scarcely satisfactory to those whose ambitions soar high, as should the ambitions of all designers. It would seem to be much more creditable to take our elements direct from nature, put our own construction upon them by altering them for use in accordance with our own artistic ideas and then build them up into designs.

This procedure would, therefore, exclude from our use artificial objects and foliage; and as animals and the human figure should be only sparingly used, the chief mass of elements would be drawn, therefore, from natural foliage and geometrical forms.

In drawing upon natural forms it is advisable to choose large fruit, such as apples, pears, oranges, lemons and pomegranates; small fruit, such as blackberries, mountain ash, corn, etc., is extremely difficult of expression in wood. Likewise, the larger flowers, or rather those with suitable petals, such as the rose, lily, daffodil, primrose, tulip—to mention a few—are more suitable for carving in wood than those with smaller or a more complex arrangement of petals. Remember that quite as truly great effects are obtained by the use of simple forms as by the introduction of very highly cultured and complex elements.

With regard to leaves, choose those whose shape and size will most readily lend themselves to the expression in wood of some principle of strength, or vigor, grace, or delicacy.

What is required is to take what appears to be the principal characteristic of the leaf, flower or fruit, and emphasize it by making it conform with our ideas of the principles of regularity, symmetry, rhythm and order.

Thus the thistle would be used to give expression to vigor, ruggedness and severity. The acanthus has been employed in all ages in giving expression to ideas of beauty, proportion and grace. The straight stalk, full sturdy flower and short twisting leaf of the tulip suggest strength and self-reliance. The oak, again, is expressive of strength, and can be used as its indicating symbol.

Certain foliage has been associated with particular ideas, and has been adopted because it visibly represents these ideas. Such symbolism has provided a fruitful source of supply for designing purposes.

The olive, for instance, is the symbol of peace, and is often used in the form of wreaths. The laurel has been used as the symbol both of atonement and of glory; the vine, too, will readily occur as being used for symbolical reasons. The Egyptians used the lotus as the symbol of immortality. Ivy, again, is used as being symbolical of friendship.

Throughout the choice of all elements, the *absolute*

suitability of the particular element chosen for expression in wood should be the designer's first care. It is of no use employing elements in building up designs *that are not capable of being expressed by the cut of the tool,* or that have no relation to it. Take a gouge and with it make a single cut in a piece of wood, then make a series of such cuts, employing tools of varying shapes and sizes, and make them an object of study. If an intelligent use be made of the results of such study, the designer will be able to use elements and make designs that have a distinct and definite relation to these cuts.

Some designs are conceived which are much more suitable for expression in other material than wood, and to secure the desired result the tools have to execute, literally, a series of very surprising gymnastics, so unsuited is the design to the wood.

One point which beginners in design should particularly note is that the principles of strength and vigor should be well in evidence. These principles are well marked in Egyptian ornament, so much so that they give to the whole ornament of this style a severity that is very characteristic. Gothic ornament may also be instanced as giving full expression to these principles or ideas; and the student is advised to study, wherever possible, any work of these periods he may happen to come across, either actual examples, or drawings, or photograph; and if the study is carried out intelligently, he will begin to understand and appreciate to its full extent the reason that exists for strength and vigor being considered as primary necessities.

It may be asked what is meant when we speak of these principles. They really mean this, that designs should be built or constructed upon somewhat similar lines or principles to those employed in the construction of buildings. The arrangement of the design should be such that the whole of the parts of which it is built should appear to be upholding one another and should suggest a feeling of there being in the arrangement a reserve of strength. The main lines, for instance, should be capable of sustaining the weight of any element, or group of elements, that may be built upon them. All stalks should have a free, natural curve that would suggest a capacity for holding without any undue strain the fruit or flower they carry. The fruit and flowers should be arranged so that they do not violate any natural instinct, so that they appear to be easily carried by the stalk.

In the construction of furniture it is a primary principle that all weight and strain should be conducted to a limited number of points arranged at suitable places, so that the weights and strains should, as far as possible, counteract one another and so assist in strengthening the whole construction. In similar manner should designs be arranged, so that the elements, or groups of elements, used may be so placed that their weight appears to be easily carried by the elements used as their supports.

In the designs illustrated, Fig. 101 shows a design intended as a panel for a small pulpit. It is based upon the oak, and shows both the leaves and acorns; it is not intended to have much surface work in modeling the leaves, the elements or individual parts being enough cut up by the broken outline; this makes it possible to treat the surface quite simply. This may be taken note of, that if the outline of any member be much indented or broken, as in this example, the surface work may be quite slight and can present a fairly smooth surface. If, on the other hand, the outline is fairly continuous, as in most parts of Fig. 103, then the

FIG. 101.

surface may be cut up in inverse ratio; this, be it understood, is a *general* rule only and is not invariably applicable to all cases.

Fig. 102 shows a design based on the tulip, arranged somewhat in modern style. It suggests how an irregularly shaped space may be filled. In this case the shape of the space partly suggests the general arrangement of the design. Many designs of this kind are so grotesquely arranged as to be quite devoid of

FIG. 102.

strength. This is so with many designs sent over from Europe, the sole aim of which appears to have been to introduce as many fantastic and grotesque curves and corners in the design as possible. Restraint has been insisted upon in previous chapters, but it may again be referred to here as being absolutely necessary to good design. Without its influence our work can easily degenerate into mere extravagant absurdity.

Fig. 103 shows an arrangement of shamrock leaves, used partly because of their natural beauty and partly because of their national significance. The arrange-ment of the stalks may be pointed out in this design. They are all there for a definite pur-pose, and not one is introduced without ful-filling some useful end. It is sometimes a great temptation to the be-ginner to fill up a space with an element that does not bear a reason-able relation to the rest of the design. It is merely used to "fill up." This should be guarded against.

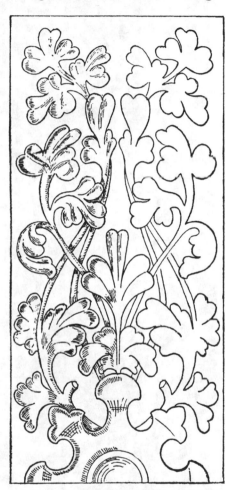

FIG. 103.

Fig. 104 gives a pho-tograph of a design which has been carved. The reason it is given is to point out two de-fects which should be avoided.

The first and most important d e f e c t is that the whole of the foliage, forming nearly the whole of each quarter, is borne upon a very inadequate support, giving the impression of weakness and insecurity. There should have been some other arrangement whereby

FIG. 104.

the foliage in question should have had a stronger and more substantial support. Another defect is in the radiation; the imperfect nature of this is evident in several places, and the attention of the student is directed to this point. There are also two elements introduced in this design that have no relation to the rest and have obviously been introduced to "fill up."

Another example of rounded work is shown in Fig. 105, but which is only given as a suggestion for a design to be made by yourself. It is a fundamental principle that both design and execution should be the work of one and the same person, and I want you to begin by strictly practicing this rule. It was indeed one of the main conditions of production in the best times of the past, and there is not a shadow of doubt that it must again come to be the universal rule if any real progress is to be made in the art of wood carving, or in any other art, for that matter. Just think for a moment how false must be the position of both parties when one makes a "design" and another carries it out. The "designer" sets his head to work (we must not count his hands at present, as they only note down the result in a kind of writing), a "design" is produced and handed over to the carver to execute. He, the carver, sets his hands and eyes to work to carry out the other man's ideas, or at least interpret his notes for the same, his head meanwhile having very little to do further than transfer the said notes to his hands. For very good reasons such an arrangement as this is bound to come to grief. One is, that no piece of carving can properly be said to be "designed" until it is finished to the last stroke. A drawing is only a map of its general outline, with perhaps contours approximately indicated by shading. In any case, even if a full-size model were supplied by the designer,

FIG. 105.

the principle involved would suffer just the same degree of violence, for it is in the actual carving of the wood that the designer should find both his inspiration and the discipline which keeps it within reasonable bounds. He must be at full liberty to alter his original intention as the work develops under his hand.

Draw and trace your outline in the same manner as before, and transfer it to the wood. You may make it any convenient size, say on a board 18 inches long by 9 inches wide, or what other shape you like, provided you observe one or two conditions which I am going to point out. It shall have a fair amount of background between the features, and the design, whatever it is, shall form a traceable likeness to a pattern of some description; it shall have a rudimentary resemblance to nature, without going into much detail; and last, it shall have a few *rounded* forms in it, rounded both in outline and on the surface, as, for instance, plums.

In setting to work to carve this exercise, follow the same procedure as in previous ones up to the point

FIG. 106.

when the surface decorations began. In the illustration there is a suggestion for a variety in the background which does not occur in the other. In this case the little branches are supposed to lie along the tops of gentle elevations and the plums to lie in the hollows. It produces a section something like this, Fig. 106. There is a sufficient excuse for this kind of treatment in the fact that the branches do not require much depth, and the plums will look all the better for

a little more.   The depth of the background will thus
vary, say between $\frac{3}{16}$ inch at the branches and $\frac{3}{8}$ inch
at the plums.   The branches are supposed to be per-
fectly level from end to end, that is, they lie parallel
to the surface of the wood, but of course curve about
in the other direction.   The leaves, on the other hand,
are supposed to be somewhat rounded and falling
away towards their sides and points in places.   The
vein in the center of the leaves may be done with a
parting tool, as well as the serrations at the edge, or
the latter may perhaps be more surely nicked out with
a chisel after the leaves have received their shapes, the
leaves being made to appear as if one side was higher
than the other and as though their points, in some
cases, touched the background, while in others the
base may be the lowest part.   The twigs coming out
from the branches to support the plums should be
somewhat like this in section, and should lie along
the curve of the background and be in themselves
rounded, as in Fig. 107; see section *aa*.   The bottom

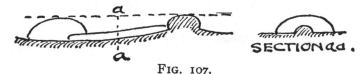

FIG. 107.

of the panel shows a bevel instead of a hollow border;
this will serve to distinguish it as a starting point for
the little branches which appear to emerge from it like
trees out of the ground.   The plums should be carved
by first cutting them down in outline to the background, as A, Fig. 108.   Then the wood should be
removed from the edge all round, to form the rounded
surface.   To do this, first take the large gouge and
with its hollow side to the wood cut off the top, from

about its middle to one end, and reversing the process do the same with the other side. Then it will appear something like B, Fig. 108. The remainder must be shaped with any tool which will do it best. There

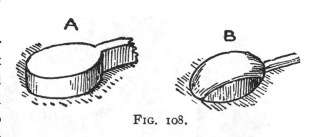

FIG. 108.

is no royal road to the production of these rounded forms, but probably gouge No. 1 will do the most of it.

Here it may be observed that the fewer tools used the better, as if many are used there is always a risk of unpleasant facets at the places where the various marks join each other. Before you try the plums, or apples, or other rounded fruit which you may have in your design, it would be as well to experiment with one on a piece of spare wood, in order to decide upon the most suitable tools. The stems or branches may be done with flat gouge No. 1, or the flat or corner chisel. A very delicate twist or spiral tendency in their upward growth will greatly improve their appearance; a mere faceting produced by a flat gouge or chisel will do this; anything is better than a mere round and bare surface, which has a tendency to look doughy. The little circular mark on the end of the plum (call it a plum, although that fruit has no such thing) is done by pressing No. 7 into the wood first, with the handle rather near the surface of the wood, and afterwards at a higher inclination, this taking out a tiny chip of a circular shape and leaving a V-shaped groove.

The number of tools referred to in the foregoing are those numbered and shown as Figs. 37 and 38.

FIG. 109.

From a comparison of the Byzantine capital, Fig. 109, with the treatment shown in Fig. 110, it will be seen how an increasing desire for imitative resemblance takes the place of a patterned foundation, and how, in consequence, the background is no longer discernible as a contrasting form. Fig. 110 is, of course, little more than a pattern with sunk holes for a background, and it is in marble; but those holes are arranged in a distinct and orderly fashion. The other is a highly realistic treatment of foliage, the likeness to nature being so fully developed that some of these groups have veins on the *backs* of the leaves. The question for the moment is this, which of the two extremes gives the clearest account of itself at a distance? We think there can be little doubt that the more formal arrangement bears this test better than the other, and this, too, in face of the fact that it has cost much less labor to produce. Remember

FIG. 110.

we are only now considering the question of *visibility* in the design. You may like the undefined and suggestive masses into which the leaves and shadows of the Gothic one group themselves better than the unbending severity of the lines in the other, but that is not the point at present. You cannot *see* the actual work which produced that mystery, and we may point out to you that what is here romantic and pleasing, on account of its changeful and informal shadows, is on the verge of becoming mere bewildering confusion; a tendency which always accompanies attempts to imitate the accidental or informal grouping of leaves so common to their natural state. The further this is carried the less is it possible to govern the forms of the background pattern; they become less discernible as contrasting *forms*, although they may be very interesting as elements of mystery and suggestive of things not

FIG. III.

actually seen. The consequence is a loss of power in producing that instantaneous impression of harmony which is one of the secrets of effectiveness in carving. This is greatly owing to the constant change of plane demanded by an imitative treatment, as well as the want of formality in its background. The lack of restful monotony in this respect creates confusion in the lights, making a closer inspection necessary in order to discern the beauty of the work. Now the human imagination loves surprises and never wholly forgives the artist who, failing to administer a pleasant shock, invites it to come forward and examine the details of his work in order to see how well they are executed.

These examples, you will say, are from architectural details which have nothing to do with wood carving. On the contrary, the same laws govern all manner of sculpturesque composition—scale or material making no difference whatever. A sculptured marble frieze or a carved ivory snuffbox may be equally censurable as being either so bare that they verge on baldness and want of interest, or so elaborate that they look like layers of fungus.

Do not imagine that we are urging any preference for a Byzantine treatment in your work; to do so would be as foolish as to ask you to don mediæval costume while at work, or assume the speech and manners of the tenth century. It would be just as ridiculous on your part to affect a bias which was not natural to you. We are, however, strongly convinced that in the choice of natural forms and their arrangement into orderly masses (more particularly with regard to their appearance in silhouette against the ground), and also in the matter of an economical use of detail, we have much to learn from the carvers who preceded the fourteenth century. They thoroughly understood and appreciated the value of the light which fell upon their work, and in designing it arranged every detail with the object of reflecting as much of it as possible. To this end, their work was always calculated for its best effects to be seen at a fairly distant point of view; and to make sure that it would be both visible and coherent, seen from that point, they insisted upon some easily understood pattern which gave the key to the whole at a glance. To make a pattern of this kind is not such an easy matter as it looks. The forms of the background spaces are the complementary parts of the design, and are just as important as those of the solid portions; it takes them both to make a good design.

Now we believe you must have had enough of this subject for the present, more especially as you have not yet begun to feel the extraordinary difficulty of making up your mind as to what is and what is not fit for the carver's uses amongst the boundless examples of beauty spread out for our choice by Dame Nature.

Meantime we do not want you to run away with the impression that, when you have mastered the principles of economy in detail and an orderly disposition of background, you have therefore learned all that is necessary in order to go on turning out design after design with the ease of a cook making pancakes according to a recipe. You will find by experience that all such principles are good for is to enforce clearness of utterance, so to speak, and to remind you that it is light you are dealing with and upon which you must depend for all effects; also that the power of vision is limited. Acting upon them is quite another matter, and one, we are afraid, in which no one can help you much. You may be counseled as to the best and most practical mode of expressing your ideas, but those thoughts and inventions must come from yourself if they are to be worth having.

We illustrate herewith two fragments of a kind of running ornament. Fig. 111 is a part of the jamb moulding of a church in Vicenza. If you observe carefully you will find that it has a decidedly classical appearance. The truth is that it was carved by a Gothic artist late in the fourteenth century, just after the Renaissance influence began to make itself felt. It is an adaptation by him of what he remembered having seen in his travels of the new style, grafted upon the traditional treatment ready to his hand. It suits our purpose all the better on that account, for the reason that we are going to re-adapt his design to an exercise and shall attempt to make it suitable to our limited ability in handling the tools, to the change in material from stone to wood, and lastly, to our different aim and motives in the treatment of architectural ornament. Now do all this for yourself in another design, and look upon this suggestion merely in the light of helping a lame dog over a stile.

In this exercise, Fig. 112, you will repeat all you have already done with the others, until you come to the shaping of the leaves, in which an undulating or up and down motion has been attempted. This involves a kind of double drawing in the curves, one for the flat and one for the projections; so that they may appear to glide evenly from one point to the other, sweeping up and down, right and left, without losing their true contours. Carvers call this process "throwing about," *i.e.*, making the leaves, etc., appear to rise from the background and again fall towards it in all directions. The phrase is a very meager one and but poorly expresses the necessity for intimate sympathy between each surface so "thrown about."

FIG. 112.

It is precisely in the observance of this last quality that effects of richness are produced. You can hardly have too much monotony of surface, but may easily err by having too much variety. Therefore, whatever system of light and shade you may adopt, be careful to repeat its motive in some sort of rhythmic order all over your work; by no other means can you make it rich and effective at a distance.

It is well every now and then to put your work up on a shelf or ledge at a distance and view it as a whole; you will see which parts tell and which do not, and so gain experience on this point. Work should also be turned about frequently, sidewise and upside down, in order to find how the light

affects it in different directions. Of course you must
not think that because your work may happen to look
well when seen from a little way off, it does not matter
about the details, whether they be well or poorly carved.
On the contrary, unless you satisfy the eye at both points
of view, your work is a partial failure. The one thing is
as important as the other, only as the first glance at
carved work is generally taken at some little distance,
it is the more immediately necessary to think of that
before we begin to work for a closer inspection. First
impressions are generally lasting with regard to carved
work, and, as we have said before, beauty of detail
seldom quite atones for failure in the arrangement of
masses.

The rounded forms in this design may give you a
little trouble, but practice, and that alone, will enable
you to overcome this. Absolute smoothness is not
desirable. Sandpapered surfaces are extremely ugly,
because they obtrude themselves on account of their
extreme smoothness, having lost all signs of handi-
work in the tool marks. Almost every beginner has
some vague impression that his first duty should be to
aim at originality. He hears eulogiums passed upon
the individuality of some one or other, and tries hard
to invent new forms of expression or peculiarities of
style, only resulting in most cases in new forms of
ugliness, which it seems is the only possibility under
such conscious efforts after novelty. The fact is that
it takes many generations of ardent minds to accom-
plish what at first each thinks himself capable of doing
alone. True originality has somewhat the quality of
good wine, which becomes more delightful as time
mellows its flavor and imparts to it the aroma which
comes of long repose; like the new wine, too,

originality should shyly hide itself in dark places until maturity warrants its appearance in the light of day. That kind of originality which is strikingly new does not always stand the test of time, and should be regarded with cautious skepticism until it has proved itself to be more than the passing fashion or novelty of a season. There is a kind of sham art, very conspicuous at the present date, popularly believed to be very original. It seems to have arisen out of some such impatient craving for novelty, and it has been encouraged by an easy-going kind of suburban *refinement* which neither knows nor cares very much what really goes to the making of a work of art. This new art has filled our stores and exhibitions with an invertebrate kind of ornament which certainly has the doubtful merit of "never having been seen before." It has evidently taken its inspiration from the trailing and supine forms of floating seaweed, and revels in the expression of such boneless structure. By way of variety it presents us with a kind of symbolic tree, remarkable for more than archaic flatness and rigidity. Now this kind of "originality" is not only absolutely valueless, but exceedingly harmful; its only merit is that, like its ideal seaweed, it has no backbone of its own, and we may hope that it will soon betake itself to its natural home—the slimy bottom of the ocean of oblivion.

Meantime, the only thing we are absolutely sure of in connection with that much abused word "originality" is this, that no gift, original or otherwise, can be developed without steady and continuous practice with the tools of your craft.

An exceedingly good example for practice is the panel shown in Fig. 113, which is drawn on a larger

scale than most of the preceding examples. It will
require considerable skill to do this piece of work

FIG. 113.

justice. Some very careful modeling will be necessary,
for on this, rather than on the depth of the work, the
beauty of the design will depend. The leaves must

be accurately outlined and then sharpness emphasized by undercutting. The stem should have particular attention paid to it to give it a "woody" character, and this may be done with a riffler or by slightly roughening it with the sharp corner of a chisel. If the panel is to be carved in a small size, box or some other fine w o o d which i s capable of taking a high degree of finish will be very appropriate. If enlarged, the panel will look well in oak.

It is usual to g i v e the novice much advice as to the way the tools should be held, but really very little that is likely to help him can be told. The most convenient way in which to do so can only be learnt by

Fig. 114.

Fig. 115.

practice, for the movements are constantly varying. As a rule, very little can be done with one hand only. Both hands must hold the tool; one, the right, supplying the force, the other being mainly used to guide and restrain.

Having now a fair idea how to do general carving,

rounded examples requiring somewhat different treatment and more experience may be given, merely remarking that the object of the accompanying designs is not so much to give detailed copies as to guide the novice.

Fig. 114 represents a handle for a paper-knife. Should the carver spoil it, neither the time nor the outlay is sufficiently serious to make the loss of any moment. The size of the wood required is 13 inches long, 1¾ inches wide and ¾ inch thick. The effect is extremely good carved either in ebony, sandalwood, or box.

Having sawed the wood to the required size, examine it carefully to make quite sure that it is sound; then, being satisfied on that point, proceed to mark the design on it as already explained. If ebony or any dark wood be used, the outline is not easily perceived, and it will therefore be necessary to draw the design on thinnish paper, and gum or paste this upon the wood itself, taking care that every part of the paper adheres thoroughly. When the paper and wood are both quite dry, fix the wood tightly into the vise and begin to work on the blade of the knife with a spokeshave. It must be scraped down gradually and circumspectly, first on one side and then on the other, taking great care not to shave it away too much in one place; the edge of the blade should run in a perfectly straight line with the handle, or it will not balance. To ensure this it is well to mark three lines down the edge of the blade before any wood is shaved off; one line should be exactly in the middle to represent the sharp cutting edge when finished, and the two others one on each side, rather less than an eighth of an inch from the center one; then, either with the saw or the spokeshave, cut away the wood down to these two outer lines and roughly shape out the form of the blade; then leave it until the time comes for finishing it off, which will be when the handle is about three parts done, when a rasp or coarse file may be used to get it into shape. Files are better than any tools for the purpose, as with them the blade can be gradually reduced without fear of spoiling it by taking off too much. The edge of broken glass will also be found very useful for the same purpose. The blade of a large paper-knife, such as this, ought, when finished, to be one-third of an inch in thickness in the thickest part, that is, where it joins the handle; from there it should slope gradually and easily down to the point and cutting edges; these latter should be perfectly free from notches in the wood, or unevenness of any kind, nor should they be over sharp or they will soon split and break off.

So to return to the handle, which has been left untouched, saving the design gummed or traced upon it. The first thing required is to cut away carefully all the waste wood in between the coils of the snake on the outside. Make the identations exactly at right angles with the surface of the design, or you will get into trouble when carving the reverse or under-side. Having done this, take the drill and make one or more holes, according to the space, in each part which requires perforation, though if preferred this part of the work may be done with a fret saw. Then, with a knife, or if the wood be fixed in a vise, with a chisel, trim the edges away nearly, but not quite, up to the inked edge of the design. When this has been done roughly, go over it again, marking slightly but distinctly where the different parts of the snake cross each other. When the general idea and shape have been thus given, examine it carefully in detail and ask, before proceeding further, such questions as, "Is this part right?" "Does that coil lie naturally?" "Am I leaving too much here, or cutting away too much there?" and so forth; do not dash and slash at it, but *think* in this manner as the work proceeds, and work gradually and cautiously up to the desired end. A good carver is always thinking in this manner, and never does a stroke without a good reason, for carving and sculpture are not like painting or even modeling, where a false stroke can be obliterated; for, a little splinter once nicked off, the snake is gone for good and the reptile looks wrong and woodeny for the rest of its days. Having fashioned it carefully but roughly in the manner described, take a coarsish file over it, guarding particularly against cutting away too much for fear of making it look attenuated, remembering that the size of the body is very considerably reduced by cutting and marking the scales, so that before this process is commenced it should look unnaturally plump and fat; and also bear in mind that in life the coils of the snake in crossing yield equally the one to the other, falling together and flattening each other, as it were, with an undulating appearance, and not crossed as so many sticks. Beginners are very apt to fail in this point. To obtain at once a correct idea, which is very essential for the execution of a lifelike carving, we strongly advise the carver to copy from life. This rule applies always when carving from nature, whether animate or inanimate, but is especially necessary to observe in regard to the former. Five minutes' examination would be of more service to the carver than a whole chapter of descriptions and directions. When the form has been cut out with tolerable accuracy, go over it all with a file fine enough to render the surface smooth, but not polished. The scales must be marked with a pencil or scratched with a fine point, an inch or so of the body at a time if the pencil be used, or the marks will rub out. For cutting them, use either the sharp point of a knife or gouges of the right size. From the size and form of the scales varying in each turn, it is necessary if the gouges are used to be constantly changing from one size to another. It is of importance to recollect that not only does each ½ inch of the reptile vary in size, increasing from the head to the middle and decreasing in like manner towards the tail, but also that the size of the scales increases and decreases in the same proportion. Moreover, that on the inner parts of the curve they are small and short, and in the outside exactly the reverse, that is, large and elongated, stretched out as it were. When the scales have been roughly denoted, rectify mistakes and irregularities; and again go over the whole, this time more carefully, and trim and shape the edges, obliterating tool marks, and define each separate scale so that they all lie equally and lightly the one over the other. This done, the paper-knife may be considered as finished, and only requires polishing. For this purpose very fine glasspaper, which has been already well worn, may be used.

To carve Fig. 115, the same directions as above should be observed as regards the blade and the snake which is twisted round the branch. This design is somewhat more difficult, but has an admirable effect when well carved. In preparing the wood, allowance must be made for the extra thickness; in fact, the part for the handle must be nearly square; about 1½ inches each way would not be too much, as it is always better to allow rather over than under the measurements required. As regards the branch round which the snake is coiled, there will be no difficulty in finding a natural model (a little spray of oak or thorn is the best for the purpose); the design will indicate where the knots and branches shall spring from the main stem, but the natural model will teach the peculiar angle and form they take better than can be given in the drawings. In so minute a piece of carving as this the bark can be very successfully imitated by wriggling the edge of a flattish gouge or chisel, held nearly uprightly, along the surface of a branch. This conveys the idea of irregularity and roughness.

FIG. 116.

Fig. 116 is another paper-knife design, also very effective and not a little quaint, which to some people is no inconsiderable recommendation. It should be carved in ebony, as it looks better in that wood than in any other. It takes a very solid piece, from 12 to 13 inches long and 1¾ inches square, for the handle. This is rather thicker than absolutely necessary, but it is well to be on the safe side. The principal point to bear in mind is that the bird be balanced well and naturally on its perch, and not appear to cling on to it by its tail. The mere roughing out is very easily done. The same care must be bestowed on the blade, which should, if anything, be somewhat thicker, to correspond with the extra thickness of the handle. The feathers are the only difficult parts; the breast should not be smooth, as it is with some birds, but ruffled and lumpy here and there. Owls are always untidy in this respect. It must be clothed with fluff, which, being of an indefinite substance, is best given by the wriggling motion of the tool described above. This gives that disheveled appearance of the feathers peculiar to the owl when disturbed and awakened in daylight and obliged to open its eyes. The latter must be set very deeply in two saucers of fluffy feathers, which set out from the eyes like fans, and should be done in the same manner as the breast feathers, with the addition of a few touches of a knife here and there to give decision. The eyes themselves should be left prominent and round, like beads, and polished brightly. The wings and tail feathers should be carefully drawn and marked out with a very small gouge, and ought to lie over each other lightly at the back; a model might be bought and thus a faithful copy made from nature— a stuffed one will answer the purpose quite as well as if it were alive. The claws must be slightly exagger-

FIG. 117.

ated and highly polished; as also the bill, which must be high and hooked and sunk deeply into the breast fluff.

The two antique examples of spandrels shown in Figs. 117 and 118 are designed for practice. Fig. 117 represents a piece of "antique" foliage carving, which is both easy and effective. Fig. 118 is of a more recent type, and is given chiefly

FIG. 118.

to suggest that similar small bits may frequently be introduced with good effect in articles of which the carving is mainly based on older styles.

The example shown in Fig. 119 offers a fine opportunity for good practice and the design is classic and

FIG. 119.

well proportioned. There is both round and flat carving in it. The animal portion is exceedingly spirited, and the leaves, which take somewhat of acanthus forms, are tastefully displayed.

CHAPTER VI

FIGURE CARVING

Our frontispiece represents a figure that is supposed to be the oldest carved wooden figure in the world, being at least 6,000 years old. It measures 3 feet 8½ inches high, and is carved in sycamore, and stands on a base of the same material, and is preserved in the Gizeh Museum, Cairo, Egypt. This famous wooden statue is known as the "Sheik-el-Belad," that is, the chief of the village, a name which the Arabs who found it bestowed on it because its features closely resembled those of their own particular Sheik. The statue is distinctly a portrait, and is generally supposed to represent one of the overseers of workmen and slaves, originally engaged in building the pyramids which abound in the district where it was discovered, and which recent "finds" have gone to prove are the oldest of all the pyramids of Egypt.

Figure carving and figure carvers have always been held in high esteem since history began, and this fact has tended to make the carver have an exalted opinion of himself, so much so that as a rule he has begun to think himself something superior to other workmen and usually turns up his nose in contempt when brought in contact with the lower grades of craftsmanship. Quoting from a recent contribution by Harry Hems, we get the following on this subject:

"In my opinion there does not exist a more conceited set of men than figure carvers. Here is a rough sketch of one taken (Fig. 120), I believe, from an old illumination dated A.D. 1452, which seems to show that in this respect they do not differ from the crafts-men of four or five centuries ago.

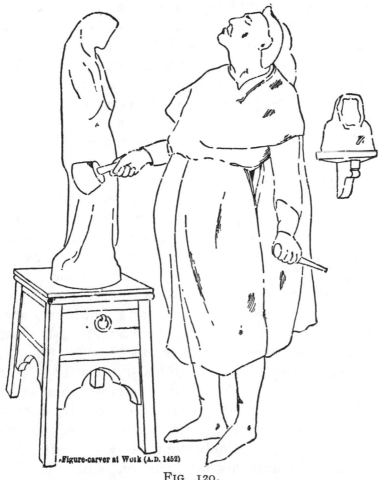

Figure-carver at Work (A.D. 1452)

FIG. 120.

"In the forty-fourth chapter of the Book of Isaiah, the following account of the figure carver's work is given: 'The carpenter stretcheth out his rule; he marketh it out with a line; he fitteth it with planes, he marketh it out with the compass, and maketh it after the figure of a man, according to the beauty of a man; that it may remain in the house. . . .'

"If a carpenter of to-day were to assay to carve a statue in wood, would he not work upon precisely the same lines? We can fancy him squaring up his stuff, putting the rule over it—chalk-lining it, perhaps— measuring it, and then making some sort of a halting start. A real figure carver, of course, after carefully modeling his proposed statue in clay, would simply put a bench screw in the back or base of the block of wood to be carved and, having secured it tightly in an upright position, level with the eye, without the least marking or measuring, would hammer away till further orders, trusting entirely to inspiration. 'What drawing are you copying?' is the constant and perhaps natural query asked by visitors to a wood carver's studio of those busily engaged in modeling or carving the figure. 'Copying nothing,' is the cool and perhaps somewhat indignant reply. 'But surely,' the enquirer will add, 'surely you are not making that lovely angel out of your own head?' 'No,' he may retort, 'my head is not a clump of wood, and that is.'

"Isaiah's carpenter cried to his statue after he made it, and said pleadingly, 'Deliver me, for thou art my god'; and to-day, although we do not actually worship, in a superstitious sense, the creations of our own brains, there is no doubt that our works oftentimes make deep impressions upon the minds of others."

No doubt there is much truth in what Mr. Hems says concerning the "conceit" of recognized figure carvers, but then they have good reason to feel proud of themselves and of their work, for it is not stretching the truth to say that among the eighty millions of people

who own these United States there is not more than
one in every million who may be considered a good
figure carver; so, if in this broad land there are not
more than eighty persons deserving the name of good
figure carvers, these eighty immortals have some good
reason to feel proud.

Like everything else where greatness is attained, the
noted figure carver is born, not made. If the divine
stuff is not in him no amount of training or practice
can possibly make a famous figure carver, but ordinary
mortals may readily attain an ordinary expertness
and be able to turn out ordinary work—the kind of
work that suits the ordinary world—which, after all,
is the most appreciated by the great mass of the
people.

Figure carving and the representation of the human
form, either in relief or in statues, is without doubt
the highest branch of the wood carver's art, and we
have for this reason deferred any remarks respecting it
until this chapter.

There are many difficulties to be mastered and
disappointments to be borne before the beginners will
be able to represent accurately in wood the "human
form divine." Generally speaking, it will be found
advisable in both animal and figure carving to con-
ventionalize the design to a certain extent. We find
frequent examples of this style of decoration in the
Greek style, where figures and animals are represented
with their extremities finished in leafage and scroll
work. There are numerous cases in which the human
form treated in a conventional manner may be
judiciously and effectively introduced among other
decorative features, either to give a symbolical meaning
or to enable the wood carver to obtain a more extended

area for the exercise of his skill than can be obtained by the use of foliated forms alone.

In the earliest ages of ornament we find figures and animals introduced to give variety to ornamentation, but they are in nearly all cases intermixed with foliage forms. In the Greek style examples often occur of the human figure being introduced in an ornamented as well as a "sculpturesque" manner in combination with scroll foliage, and the Roman carried the principle still further by combining the figure with the foliage itself.

Fig. 121.

The practice of introducing animals, birds and grotesque figures in order to give life and variety to ornamentation has been a common one with most designers, both ancient and modern, and in the Renaissance style such combinations occur frequently, examples of which are given in Figs. 119 and 121. Before proceeding to describe the method to be adopted in the carving of these designs, I wish to give a few hints respecting the introduction by the amateur of animal forms in his designs. There need be no limit to the formation and designing of either the conventional animal forms or the grotesque, provided the ordinary laws of good taste be not infringed. For instance, if grotesque or animal forms are introduced into the design, either by combining the monsters in the scrolls or by placing the animals upon the tendrils of plants, it is obviously necessary to proportion them accordingly. Besides figures, a good many other forms have from time to time been introduced as aids to decorations; and in many examples of Grinling Gibbons' work, not only dead game, but also the implements of the chase have been introduced, although, perhaps, this can hardly be termed or considered a high-class method of ornamentation. In the examples shown in Figs. 119 and 121 the human and other forms are in combination with foliage, etc. In this description of work the same process is gone through as previously described, is traced on the surface of the wood, then roughly "blocked" in with a quick tool, taking particular care to preserve a few points to work by. In carving any piece of work, however, which involves a great amount of labor and is in high relief, we should most strongly advise the beginner to model the design first of all in clay, so as to get a general idea of the effect; or, if clay is not available, cut in the design roughly in any soft wood, such as pine. This advice may at first sight appear to entail a great amount of additional labor, but in the end the extra work will be amply repaid, as the work will be facilitated in every way.

In carving figures of animals, birds, reptiles, it is best, if possible, to have an actual figure or animal as a model, as a dog's head or a dead robin suspended on the slab by a large-headed nail, of course an imitation one carved out of the solid wood. There are few more beautiful subjects for the carver than this of dead birds, and it is one which can be used in a variety of manners, either purely as an ornament to lay on a slab, or to hang up against the wall, or as a panel for a cabinet or sideboard. For the latter purpose half relief will be sufficient; for the former, three-quarters, or even entire relief, is desirable. It were useless for us to attempt to give any design of this description, for nothing short of a photograph or a most minute engraving could delineate the description and texture of the feathers; but this, however, is of little importance, as the natural bird is about the best model that can be had, and this is within reach of every one; but we would remind all those who intend to study from models of this kind, that it is preferable to do so in the winter, for not only will it longer retain its original pose, but the worker will not be tempted to hurry over his work for unsavory reasons. All difficulties of this kind, however, may be avoided, and skill in carving materially improved if a slight knowledge of modeling in clay be attained. Of course, in speaking thus we mean modeling in its simplest forms, merely enough to enable us to retain forms in our memory for future use, which either by nature or circumstances are fleeting; such, for instance, as a specially beautiful group of leaves or flowers, which, even could they be gathered without destroying their pose, would wither before they could be expressed in wood; or, again, to return to the case in point, modeling is invaluable to enable the artist to catch the general outline of a bird, or a group of birds or animals, while they are still fresh, before they become stark and stiff; the feathering or fur, being a detail, can be copied from models of the same kind, placed as nearly as possible in the same position. It may be argued that a slight pencil sketch would answer the purpose as well as a clay model, and with less expenditure of time and trouble, but it is not so, for a few skillful touches in clay will convey an idea such as would be useful to the carver far better than could be done with the pencil, unless it were in very talented hands; moreover, as the rudiments of carving and modeling are the same (which is not the case as regards drawing), it is probable that to express an idea in clay would be easier to the carver than to do so by means of the pencil.

A good quantity of modeling clay can be bought for a mere trifle. It can usually be procured at any pottery works, from pipe makers, or at cast shops; but in this latter place it is generally more expensive. It is sold in the form of powder mixed with rough lumps; these must be thoroughly crushed, and the powder worked up with water into a smooth dough, which should be as stiff and dry as is compatible with its being easily handled, for the moister it is so much the greater will be the risk of its cracking when the water evaporates. In many cases ordinary clay will answer, if properly managed. The model, when you are not at work on it, should be kept damp with a wet handkerchief or rag thrown over it; if this precaution be neglected, it will dry unevenly and fall to pieces. The same clay can be broken up and used over and over again by taking care to grind it finely before mixing it afresh. The few tools and instruments required for modeling are very simple and inexpensive, merely little sticks of wood or ivory with different-shaped knobs at the end, others, again, being pointed and curved. Half a dozen of the ordinary shapes would do to start with, and with the aid of a knife and some glasspaper a modeler could easily make as many others as necessity or fancy suggested, the chief point being to make them very smooth, that the clay may not adhere to them. Plaster of Paris, though not so artistic, is not a bad substitute for clay; it must be ground and mixed in the same manner, but it must be used with more water, as it sets quickly and soon dries. It can then be cut or scraped with a knife or tool, and should a mistake occur it can be easily remedied by adding a fresh daub of the plaster.

The next design, Fig. 122, is an eagle for a lectern.

The original carving from which this drawing is taken was executed chiefly from nature. It measures 4 feet across the wings and stands 4 feet 4 inches high, irrespective of the stand on which it is placed. This is, however, an unusually large size, it being intended for a

Fig. 122.

cathedral; from 22 to 30 inches across the wings are the usual dimensions. Before commencing this or any large work of a similar nature, it is advisable to make a small working model of the subject; this model should be made to scale, that is, it should bear a certain proportion to the large work, as, for instance, should it be proposed to make the eagle 24 inches across, then let the model be 8 inches, that is, 4 inches

to the 1 foot. It need not, of course, be highly
finished, the minor details of feathering, claws, etc.,
being of no account, as the sole object is to arrive at
a just idea of the general effect, and to satisfy yourself
that the pose and proportions are correct before commencing on the wood itself; of course, should you
copy from a model the size of your own carving, these
preliminaries will not be necessary; it is only when
you are called upon either to greatly increase or reduce
its proportions that this extra work is advisable. A
very expert carver might even dispense with it
altogether, but it would be extremely rash in a novice to do
so, for, as we have elsewhere
remarked, carving cannot be
altered at will, not at least to
any extent; therefore the greater caution used, so much the
greater will be the chance of
success.

FIG. 123.

To make a rough model,
such as described, of the eagle in Fig. 122, it will be
necessary, on account of the soft, yielding nature of
the clay, to form it on a kind of frame, a skeleton, so
to speak, which will give it strength to bear its own
weight. Fig. 123 represents such a skeleton, which
consists of five strips of wood nailed or tied firmly
together and fixed into a square of wood so as to
form a solid base on which to stand; the two side
pieces are tied strongly, as shown, to the crosspiece
in front, while the middle piece passes in front
in a slanting position, to form the slope from
the breast to the extremity of the tail; the head,
from being thrown back in the act of looking upwards,

balances and supports its own weight. Some carvers prefer to make their models, as stated before, in soft wood, such as pine or basswood, and this plan has certainly the advantage in that it is more durable than either clay or plaster, but it is not so satisfactory on the whole, as in the latter materials the form can be altered and re-altered until it is quite to the artist's mind, which cannot be the case in wood.

Be very careful in superintending the preparation of the wood, and the manner in which it is joined together. This should be entrusted only to a very skillful workman, and one who thoroughly understands his business, for the beauty and success of the work will mainly depend on the exactness and strength with which the parts are put together. Much judgment and care must be expended in the arrangement of the joins, in order that they may interfere as little as possible with the carving itself, as, for instance, the head should be in one piece, that is, with a join on either side, and not in the middle, and so on.

The wood should be cut out of the block and exposed to the air as long a time as possible before it is built up; the longer the better, as the chance of warping, which would be fatal to the work, is greatly lessened by many months' exposure. Flaws and knots in the wood itself, though by no means desirable, are comparatively of little importance, as from the boldness and freedom of the design much is left to the artist's fancy, so that any little local flaw can be worked in and concealed amongst the irregularities of the plumage. There is yet one other point which requires attention before the wood is finally clamped together, and this is to place those pieces side by side which agree the best in color and grain. The shades of the different blocks should blend together so as to give the semblance as far as may be of the eagle being carved out of one entire piece; carelessness in this respect cannot be atoned for by the finest carvings, for all the artist's skill could not save the bird from appearing patchy and woodeny if a stripe of lighter color than the rest ran down the breast. This is a misfortune which the most ignorant novice can with a little care and painstaking avoid.

In regard to the actual manual part of the subject, it is useless to lay down any rules for the carver's guidance, as it is better in these comparatively minor details that he should work in accordance with his own comfort and convenience. As a broad rule, however, it is always well to "rough out" the subject uniformly and to avoid entering into detail, so as to arrive as soon as may be at a just idea of the general effect, and afterwards to go over it again with a little more exactitude, repeating this process until it stands completed as regards the pose and main features, but devoid, in the case of the subjects in question, of plumage and such like *minutiæ*. These should then in their turn be roughly delineated and gradually be worked up together into a perfect whole. It is only by rigidly following out this plan that a uniform and natural effect can be obtained by the inexperienced workman; if, for instance, one wing were highly finished in all its points before the other was begun, the greater part would probably have to be altered, or, as very likely this would be impossible, without cutting away too much of the wood, the two wings would look as if they did not belong to the same bird and the effect of the whole carving would be spoilt. Doubtless this manner of working up the whole by slow degrees is somewhat a trial of patience, especially if it be a first work of the kind, for it certainly is very tempting to finish up a little bit in order to see the effect. This, though satisfactory for the moment, will spoil the appearance of the finished work, or at any rate is a great risk on account of the danger of cutting away too much of a particular part before it is possible to judge of the whole.

The feet and head of the eagle will require great care, especially the former. Procure, if possible, a real foot as a model. If an eagle's cannot be obtained, that of a similar bird of prey must do duty. Bestow much pains on observing and imitating the roughness of their texture and the manner in which the fluff falls over and around them. The eagle may be designed to stand on a ball of wood, or upon a rock, but be sure that you do not carve or draw a fancy rock out of your own head, for unless you are well practiced in such matters it will assuredly be stiff and conventional; but look about and find a real stone, to which, if too large to move, take your modeling clay and copy it faithfully on the spot, and afterwards at home model your eagle upon it. If the worst comes to the worst, and you cannot light on either rock or stone which is suitable, you might find a worse model for your purpose than a piece of coal, which is in every one's reach. Take care in placing the model on the rock that the claws really clutch it, and that the bird is properly poised and balanced upon it.

We will now pass on to the last and perhaps the most difficult branch of the art—that of carving in basso-relievo. For this a knowledge of drawing is almost a necessity, as is also the rudiments of perspective; we say *almost* necessary, for in some rare cases the artist's eye is so intuitively accurate that he can afford to dispense with such knowledge and may trust solely to an acute feeling of proportion and form to guide him aright; but this is very exceptional, therefore it would be well for those who intend to pursue this branch to practice drawing from cases, if obtainable, and to make the rules of perspective a preliminary study. We would especially counsel ladies to follow this particular line of art, which, while necessitating skill of the highest order, involves the expenditure of less actual strength than those carvings which are in full relief.

The student in this style has an abundance of beautiful and suitable subjects at his command, for not only are casts of most of the best works of this kind procurable, but there is also another field open to him in the many pictures and parts of pictures which are now placed within our reach by means of photography. We could not, however, counsel him to attempt to carve from a flat object, such as a picture, until he has first practiced both carving and drawing from a cast, in order to educate the eye in the perspective of figures for this especial purpose. No better models can be found than the casts from the basso-relievos of Luca della Robbia. After having worked thus from casts, the next step in advance is to do so from photographs of basso-relievo sculpture; from thence you may, if you wish, pass on to carve from photographs of pictures. Having arrived at this point, your choice of subjects is practically unlimited. Choose, to begin with, a bold and somewhat severe outline, such for instance as some of Ary Scheffer's figures; carved pictures of this kind are, when artistically executed, very beautiful; and the edge of the wood, beveled and finished with a simple ogee, is generally sufficient margin to set off the carving, or engraving similar to the one shown in Fig. 124, which shows birds, berries, butterflies, insects and foliage.   They present, when finished, the appearance of the picture of figure, being set in saucers or basins of wood, varying in depth according to the taste of the carver, and may be either round or oval, whichever is most suitable to the subject.   For small picture carvings of this kind, a flat or slightly beveled rim or velvet laid on the wall about 1 or 2 inches in width is a great improvement and sets it off wonderfully. This style of wood sculpture was much practiced in the sixteenth century, especially in Spain, where there are many specimens of the kind still preserved; these, also, in many instances, bear marks of the background having been gilded and even painted in color. Whether the latter was an improvement is, we think, questionable, but as regards the former, there is little doubt that the gilding adds considerably to the effect of the carving, as the reflection of the gold on the convex background marks the outlines and throws it into great relief.   Any good single head set thus, as it were, in a round dish or saucer of wood, would be an excellent study and form also an extremely handsome object in a room, hung picturewise on the wall; you will find some very beautiful heads suited for this purpose on the doors of the Baptistry at Florence. Excellent photographs have been taken of the original, from which a good carver could easily work.

To find good casts is a somewhat more difficult matter, especially for those who live in the country The plaster of Paris images which are offered for sale in the streets would very probably mislead rather than

FIG. 124.

guide and improve your taste, so that on the whole it would be safer and better to trust to drawings and photographs of really good works, which must be correct.

The carver will, doubtless, in many instances, find it necessary to enlarge or reduce the dimensions of his model or design, as it would be unlikely that he could find a drawing or photograph of precisely the requisite size. In this case we would advise him to adopt a mechanical plan in vogue amongst copyists, namely, to cover the face of the design with a network of horizontal and perpendicular lines by means of a light pencil or chalk; or if you do not wish to make marks on the design, stretch threads across from edge to edge in the following manner: The picture or photograph must first be fixed on a drawing-board, or, if you have not one, any soft pine board which will not warp will do as well; then mark out a square enclosing it—let us say 12 inches in size; of course, this will vary according to the dimensions of the photograph. Each inch on both sides and at the top and bottom must be exactly measured off and marked with a short steel pin or tack; strain threads first horizontally and then perpendicularly from pin to pin, then take a sheet of drawing paper of the exact size you intend your carving to be, and on it rule the same number of lines as there are threads over the photograph. You will thus have the same number of squares in each, larger or smaller, as the case may be. In each square on your drawing paper sketch in the figure, part of figure, or whatever is the subject which is enclosed in the corresponding square of the photograph. By this simple method even the most clumsy draughtsman is enabled to make a sufficiently correct outline.

In order, however, to give a clear idea of how to enlarge a drawing we submit the following method: Readers who are inexperienced in the art of draughtsmanship, and to whom "drawing to scale" is a term with a deeply mysterious meaning, naturally find it very difficult to make use of a sketch or design which happens to be many times smaller than it is intended to be carried out. The enlarging from a small sketch will be found tiresome and liable to lead to error; and again, where the beauty of the design depends on subtle curvatures and nice spacing, the inexpert will be apt to spoil the whole by injudicious touches. For all that, there is

FIG. 125.   FIG. 126.

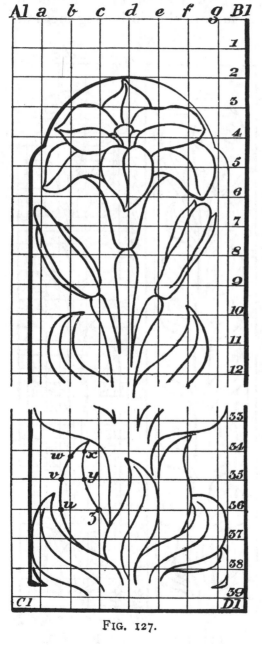

FIG. 127.

room left for the exercise of the draughtsman's art, as will presently appear.

There are four ways of enlarging a design. One is the method of enlarging by means of squaring over the design, and another involves the use of an instrument known as the pantograph.

When speaking of 'designs" in this connection, it should be understood that ornament rather than construction is meant.

We shall deal first with that involving only the use of paper and pencil, drawing board, T-square, etc.; the method leaves some little drawing to the hand of the operator, which the pantograph does not, but few will be found unequal to the task.

and there is generally a little more "life" in the free-hand drawing than in that quite mechanically done. The example mentioned, a piece of carved ornament for a mirror frame, will serve excellently for illustration, being bold, free and simple, yet admirable in its class. It is here reproduced, Fig. 125, as original, and by its side will be seen the same design "squared over" to show the principle of enlarging by this method. Fig. 127 shows the design enlarged to three times the original, and the way this is accomplished, while it may be obvious to many, remains to be explained.

The first thing to be done is to get the outline of the extreme outside of the panel. If the drawing is to be made direct on the wood this outline will, of course, be the edges of the finished board (neglecting tenons or other purely constructional details). We are supposing the enlargement to be to three times the original; measuring this, we find the outline to be $4\frac{15}{16}$ inches (bare) by 1 inch. Multiplying each of these dimensions by three gives us the size of the finished board, $14\frac{3}{4}$ inches (say) by 3 inches. (The whole length of $14\frac{3}{4}$ inches cannot, of course, be accommodated in one of these pages, so that only half is shown. This will make no difference to the explanation.)

The next process is the division of the original drawing into a number of rectangular spaces. Any number of divisions will do, but the closer they are the more exact will be the reproduction; but if too close will prove troublesome. As the drawing is an inch wide, it will be simplest to divide the width at top and bottom into eight equal parts ($\frac{1}{8}$ inch each) and join up as shown in Fig. 126. Had the width been, say, $1\frac{1}{32}$ inches, eight divisions would still have been a very suitable amount, but the ordinary scale or rule would have been useless and a pair of compasses or dividers would have to be used to space out the divisions equally. The important point is to get all the spaces accurately alike, as on this depends the correctness of the copy.

The vertical height of the drawing has next to be divided up. There is not the least necessity to make these spaces the same as the others, so long as a convenient width can be found for them, but in the present case $\frac{1}{8}$ inch spaces *will* be found convenient, largely because this happens to be the most ordinary spacing on a two-foot or other rule. Starting from the top of the drawing at A, therefore, mark off $\frac{1}{8}$ inch spaces all the way down to C; and then do the same from B towards D. Join the marks so made so as to cover the whole drawing with a square network like Fig. 126. Use a fine-pointed hardish pencil for the purpose, and do not press too heavily; the page will not be spoiled by the process, even if the lines are not afterwards rubbed out.

It will be noticed that owing to the length of A B ($4\frac{15}{16}$ inches) not being an amount exactly divisible into eighths, a small space about $\frac{1}{16}$ inch wide is left at the bottom. Neglect this, as it will not in the least interfere with subsequent operations.

Now turn to the outline already prepared for the enlarged drawing (A1 B1, C1 D1, Fig. 127). A1 B1 and C1 D1 have to be divided into the same number of spaces as A B, C D in Fig. 126, viz., eight. Obviously these spaces will be three times the size of the others, and $\frac{1}{8}$ inch $\times 3 = \frac{3}{8}$ inch. Mark off A1 B1, therefore, at intervals of $\frac{3}{8}$ inch and do the same at the other end of the pilaster, and join up. Had A B been divided into eight parts with the dividers, owing to the impossibility of using a definite division on an ordinary rule, A1 B1 would likewise have to be divided with compasses, by trial, in the same way.

Similar proceedings have to be taken in the case of the height A1 C1. It is all plain sailing in this instance, as one has only to mark off intervals of ⅜ inch all the way down from A1 and B1 and join up. Note that at the bottom a narrow space should occur, corresponding with that at the bottom of the original. To simplify matters, number the divisions on the original, and copy in some such manner as here shown, where *1* in Fig. 126 corresponds with 1 in Fig. 127, *2* with 2, *a* with a, *b* with b, and so on.

We are now ready for transferring the drawing, the process being similar to that one learns at school for copying maps. Every point where a line in the original crosses either a horizontal or vertical line, can be located on the copy with absolute precision, and when a number of such points have been found, can be readily joined up by freehand drawing. Take the case of the point marked *z* (near the bottom of Fig. 126). This point marks a place where the drawing crosses both a vertical and horizontal line at their intersection. Following the lines along, they will be found to be No. 36 (horizontal) and *c* (vertical). Turning to Fig. 127, the intersection of 36 and *c* is easily found, and a dot should be made there, *z*. The next point on the curve of the leaf to which we are paying attention is on line 35, at *y*; this is approximately half-way between vertical lines *b* and *c*, and a similar position half-way between *b* and *c* on line 35 in Fig. 127 can easily be found; it is marked *y*. In the same way the points *x*, *w*, *v*, *u* are transferred to the larger drawing, where they are marked by corresponding letters, and so on, right through the design.

It will be found the best plan to sketch in each leaf or similar small portion of the design as soon as the points marking its position have been fixed. This will avoid the confusion likely to occur if a large area is covered with dots, which will tend to become meaningless. Thus the leaf marked out may be sketched in quite regardless of the other leaves, stalks, etc., surrounding it. At the top of the drawing the finished design is given, and it will be seen how closely this copies by the original, from which it was taken precisely by this method.

It is not generally imperative that absolute accuracy should be observed in copying; consequently the little differences due to slight aberrations of the hand when sketching in will by no means mar the work. The unpracticed amateur will do well to follow the directions given implicitly, but he will find in time that it is quite easy to do without marking any points on his enlarged drawing, simply drawing freehand, watching the original with one eye and the copy with the other, as it were. In this way a copy can be made with a very near approximation to accuracy and very quickly, all that is necessary being close attention to three lines—the drawing and the upright and horizontal lines.

While all the above may be very clear in the comparatively simple instance given, a number of slight variations may arise which are sure to puzzle a beginner. Suppose, instead of an enlargement of this simple kind, where the small drawing is to the large in the proportion of one to three, that the larger is no definite multiple of the other. To state a case, we can imagine the worker to have a panel of suitable proportions to take the design (Fig. 125), only that it happens to be, say, $4\frac{9}{16}$ inches wide. All he has to do is to divide the width into eight equal parts, by means of the dividers, taking no notice of what the actual widths are on a scale ($4\frac{9}{16} \div 8 = \frac{73}{128}$, an amount which could never be marked off with an ordinary rule with accuracy). In this case the best way to mark off the vertical heights would be to stretch the legs of the dividers accurately to the full width of the board ($4\frac{9}{16}$ inches) and mark off that amount all the way down each side. Then close up the dividers to *one* space width and mark off each of the long divisions into eight parts. If the small spacing is marked off with the dividers right away down the side without the larger spacings to guide one, errors are apt to creep in and even to get multiplied as the marking proceeds. If the side A C (Fig. 126) has been divided up into any given numbers of parts, so that these spaces are *not* the same as those along A B, all that need be done is to divide up the sides of the board into a similar number of equal parts, ignoring the spacing (A B) altogether.

It has been tacitly assumed in the above that the enlarged drawing was strictly proportionate to the other, both in width and length. It may, however, sometimes occur that the reader notes a design which he particularly desires to employ in filling a given space, which is a little too long or too wide for strict proportion. He must, of course, decide whether the disproportion is too violent, as it would never do to enlarge a drawing like Fig. 125 to, say, twice the width and three times the length; yet it would be reasonable to enlarge it to 4 inches in width and 20½ inches in length, and few would be able to discover the discrepancy. To do this, it is necessary to divide up the long side, A B in Fig. 126, not into eighths, but into any equal parts, and then to divide the 20½ inches into the same number of parts. In the present case those on A B will be slightly more than ⅛ inch each; the subsequent marking off will finish the design.

We have hitherto spoken of carving in basso-relievo merely from a secular point of view, as works of art or embellishment of a room. But this style enters also largely into ecclesiastical ornamentation, and there are few finer subjects for the carver's skill than an altar piece, reredos, or panels of a like nature. This, however, is not the place (nor, indeed, is it within the limit we have given ourselves) to enter into details as regards this special style of work. Those of our readers who intend to turn their attention to this branch of that art would do well before they undertake any work of this kind to consult with an architect, or some one well versed in such matters (unless he has studied the subject himself), and to procure a slight sketch of the style and proportions best suited to the church which he proposes to decorate, in order that his work may amalgamate with the age and architecture of the edifice.

As this book is intended purely as a guide to beginners, those designs have been chosen which we consider as especially suited to this class, rather than to the professional carver, and for this reason we have confined ourselves to drawings and description of such subjects as the amateur can execute without the intervention of much professional help from the cabinet-maker.

The main object of the beginners should be to produce artistic work in which the mere expense is secondary and kept in abeyance to pure art. With this idea in view he will have a chance of excelling, and possibly of designing and executing original work, but this he cannot hope to do if he merely follow in the footsteps and copies, however faithfully and skillfully, the works of professional furniture carvers, who, with the advantage of constant practice, combined with, perhaps, a long apprenticeship in a large workshop, will be sure to surpass the amateur in the manual part of this work, however gifted the latter may be. In all employments the professional must work in such a manner and on such subjects as will ensure good and certain wages, and not according to his own special taste. The learner has probably ample time at command and therefore should give full scope to his own artistic fancies instead of reproducing other people's ideas, for it is to him that we must look for inventiveness and imagination. Let him then follow his own special line, feeling assured that what of skill may be wanting is more than compensated by natural talent, exceeding probably by many degrees the professional carver who pursues the calling not from any special predilection, but solely through circumstances or necessities.

We now come to the question, what are we going to do with all the pieces of carving which we propose to undertake?

There is no more inexorable law relating to the use of wood carving than the one which insists upon some kind of passport for its introduction, wherever it appears. It must come in good company and be properly introduced. The slightest and most distant connection with a recognized sponsor is often sufficient, but it will not be received alone. We do not make carvings to hang on a wall and be admired altogether on their own account. They must decorate some object. A church screen, a font, a piece of furniture, or even the handle of a knife. It is not always an easy matter to find suitable objects upon which to exercise our wood carving talents. Our furniture is all made now in a wholesale manner which permits of no interference with its construction, while at the same time, if we wish to put any carving upon it, it is absolutely essential that both construction and decoration should be considered together.

A very modest beginning may be made in adapting ornament to a useful article, by carving the surface of a bread plate. These are usually made of some hard wood, such as sycamore. They may be made of oak, but sycamore has the advantage in its lighter color, which is more likely to be kept clean. A good suggestion is given in Fig. 128 for carving appropriate to this purpose. The essentials are, that there should be a well-defined *pattern*, simple in construction and as effective as possible with little labor; that there should be little or no rounding of surface, the design consisting of gouge cuts and incisions arranged to express the pattern. The incisions may form a regular sunk ground, but it should not be deep. or it will not be easily kept clean. Then, as in cutting bread the knife comes in contact with the surface, no delicate work is advisable; a large treatment with broad surfaces, and some plain spaces left to protect the carved work, is likely to prove satisfactory in every way. A piece of sycamore should be procured ready for carving; this may be got from a wood turner, out it will be as well to give him a drawing, on which is shown the section of edge and the position of all turned lines required for confining the drawing. If the plate is to be of any shape other than circular, then it must be neatly made by yourself.

Many of you are, we have no doubt, handy joiners, and may be able to put together some pieces of furniture to serve at least as an excuse for the intro-

FIG. 128.

duction of your carving. Here are some suggestions for corner cupboards, chosen as giving the largest area for carved surface with the minimum of expense in construction. The material should be oak, if possible, or it may be walnut. The doors of Figs. 129 and 130 are in three narrow boards with shallow beads at the joints, those of the others are each made of a single board and should be ½ to ⅝ inch thick; the doors

may be about 2 feet 6 inches high, each having two
ledges, about 3 inches wide, screwed on behind top

FIG. 129.   FIG. 130.

and bottom to keep them from twisting. All mouldings, beads, etc., are to be carved by hand, no planes

Half   Half

FIG. 131.   FIG. 138.

being used. Having traced the lines of your design upon the board, you may begin, if there are mouldings, as in Fig. 131, by using a joiner's marking gauge to groove out the deepest parts of the parallel lines in the mouldings along the edges, doing the same to the curved ones with a V tool or veiner. Then form the mouldings with your chisels or gouges. Keep them very flat in section, as in Fig. 133.

The fret patterns in Figs. 131, 133 and 134, where not pierced, should be done in low relief, not more than ⅛ inch deep, and the sides of the bands beveled as in section *a*, Fig. 132. The widths of these bands ought not to be less than ½ inch, and look better if they are wider. Very narrow bands have a better appearance

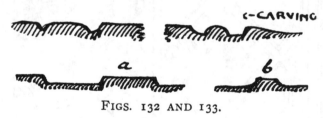

FIGS. 132 AND 133.

if, instead of being cut straight down, they are hollowed at sides like *b* in Fig. 132.

Fig. 136 is a detail of a kind of gouge work which you must know very well. One perpendicular cut of a gouge driven in with the mallet, and one side cut, should form one of these crescent or thimble-shaped holes. They should not be too deep in proportion to their size. Their combinations may be varied to a great extent. Two or three common ones are shown in the illustration. This form of ornament was in all likelihood invented by some ingenious carpenter with a turn for art and a limited stock of tools for carving. His humble contribution to the resources of the

FIG. 134.   FIG. 135.

carver's art has received its due share of the flattery which is implied by imitation. In all these patterns it is well to remember that the flat surface of the board left between the cuts is really the important thing to consider, as all variety is obtained by disposing the

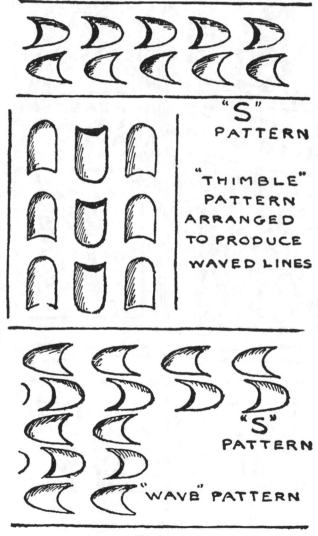

FIG. 136.

square.   This tool requires great care in sharpening, but will be found a most useful tool when in proper order.

We give illustrations of a set of jewelry consisting of a brooch and earrings, having for their decoration motive the ivy leaf.   The ebony or other material for these designs should be planed to the thickness of about a quarter of an inch, unless it is desired to make the work appear in very bold relief, when an additional

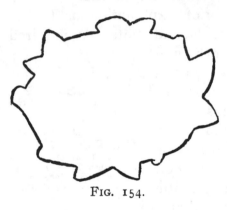

one-eighth of an inch would be required.   A piece of thin white paper should be pasted on the work and the outline to be fret cut, as in Fig. 154, traced upon it.   After being fret-cut, glue down the ebony to a piece of pine, taking care to in-

FIG. 154.

sert between the ebony and the pine a piece of brown paper.   The outline of the whole design should now be traced on the face of the brooch and the superfluous wood cut away, and the background regulated with a smaller router so as to be of uniform depth.   In setting in the outlines, care must be taken not to undercut the leaves.   When this is done, use a quick tool to rough in the leaves and to show the course of the stem, afterwards regulating the outlines of the leaves, finishing the twist of each leaf and giving a rough appearance to the stem.   Although it is impossible to exactly imitate the natural leaf and stem, still the chief characteristics should be preserved, and the amateur will find it convenient to have a few of the natural ivy leaves before holes in such a way as to produce the pattern required by means of their outlines on the plain surface. Thus waved lines are produced as in Fig. 136, and little niches like mimic architecture as in Fig. 137, by the addition of the triangular-shaped holes at the top and the splayed sills at the bottom. (It is obvious that an arrangement like the latter should never be turned upside down.) If this attention to the surface pattern is neglected the holes are apt to become mere confused and meaningless spots.

In small pieces of furniture like these, which are made of comparatively thin wood, the carving need not have much depth, say the ground is sunk ¼ inch at the deepest. As oak is more tenacious than pine, you will find greater freedom in working it, although it is so much harder to cut. You may find it necessary to use the mallet for the greater part of the blocking out, but it need not be much used in finishing. A series of short strokes driven by gentle taps of the mallet will often make a better curve than if the same is attempted without its aid.

It will be well now to procure the remainder of the set of twenty-four tools if you have not already got them, as they will be required for the foliage we are about to attempt. The deep gouges are especially useful; having two different sweeps on each tool, they adapt themselves to hollows which change in section as they advance.

Fig. 131 contains very little foliage, such as there is being disposed in small diamond-shaped spaces, sunk in the face of the doors, and a small piece on the bracket below. All this work should be of a very simple character, definite in form and broad in treatment.

Fig. 138 is more elaborate, but on much the same lines of design, varied by having a larger space filled with groups of leaves. Fig. 137 gives the carving to a larger scale; in it the oak leaves are shown with raised veins in the center, the others being merely indicated

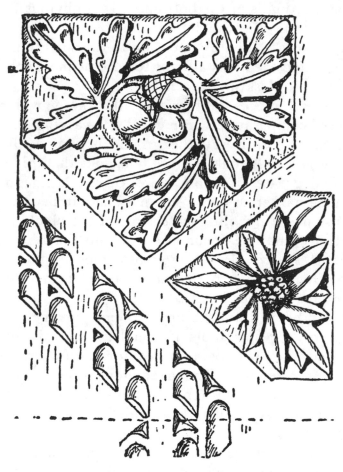

SECTION a　　SECTION b

CARVING IN PANELS

Fig. 137.

by the gouge hollows. There is some attempt in this at a more natural mode of treating the foliage. While such work is being carved, it is well to look now and then at the natural forms themselves (oak and laurel in this case), in order to note their characteristic features, and as a wholesome check on the dangers of mannerism.

It is a general axiom founded upon the evidence of past work, and a respect for the laws of construction in the carpenter's department, that when foliage appears in panels divided by plain spaces it should never be made to look as if it *grew from one panel into the other*, with the suggestion of boughs passing behind the solid parts. This is a characteristic of Japanese work and may, perhaps, be admirable when used in delicate painted decorations on a screen or other light furniture, but in carvings it disturbs the effect of solidity in the materials, and serves no purpose which cannot be attained in a much better way. Expedients have been invented to overcome the difficulty of making a fresh start in each panel, one of which is shown in Fig. 137, where the beginning of the bough is hidden under a leaf. It is presumable that the bough *may* go on behind the uncarved portions of the board, to reappear in another place, but we need not insist upon the fancy, which loses all its power when attention is called to it, like riddles when the answer is known.

In Fig. 134, like the last, the treatment is somewhat realistic. This is shown to a larger scale in Fig. 140. Nevertheless, it has all been "arranged" to fit its allotted space, and all accidental elements eliminated; such, for instance, as leaves disappearing in violent perspective, or even turned sidewise, and all minute details which would not be likely to show con-

spicuously if carved in wood. Fig. 141 is a detail
copied from nature, but which might stand without
alteration provided it formed part of a work delicate

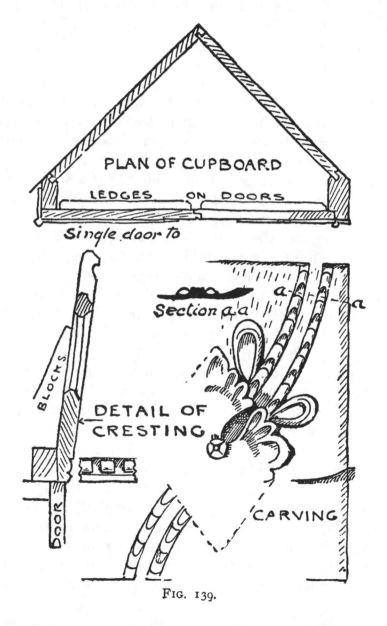

PLAN OF CUPBOARD

LEDGES ON DOORS

Single door to

Section a·a

BLOCKS

DETAIL OF
CRESTING

DOOR

CARVING

FIG. 139.

enough to note such close elaboration in so small a
space. This, of course, would entirely depend upon
the purpose for which the carving was intended, and
whether it was meant for distant view or close inspection. As there is arrangement necessary in forming
the outline, so there is just as much required in
designing the articulation of the surfaces of the leaves,

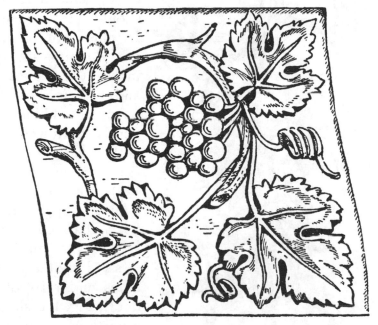

FIG. 140.

which should be so treated that their hollows fall into
a semblance of some kind of pattern.

Fig. 135 is a more formal design, or, to use a very
much abused word, more "conventional," in which
such leafage as there is only serves the purpose of
ornamental points, marking the divisions of the
general design. The gouge work upon the leaves
should be of the simplest description, but strict atten-

tion is necessary in drawing the grooves so that their forms may be clear and emphatic, leaving no doubt as to the pattern intended. Designs of this kind have no interest whatever except as pieces of patterned work, to which end every other consideration should be sacrificed. It must not be cut too deeply—say ¼ inch at the deepest— and the sides of the panels should be very gently hollowed out with a flattish sweep (see section on Fig. 139), in order to avoid any appearance of actual construction in what more or less imitates the stiles and rails of a door. Fig. 139 shows a portion of the leafage to a larger scale, and also a plan explaining the construction of all these cupboards.

Fig. 141.

Fig. 139 is designed upon the barest suggestion of natural foliage, the wavy stem being quite flat, and running out flush into the flat margins at the sides, connecting them together. The leaves in this case should be carved, leaving the veins standing solid; grooved veins would have a meager look upon such rudimentary leaves. Of course a more natural treat-

ment may be given to this kind of design, but in that case it would require to be carried all over the door and replace the formally ornamental center panel. The pierced pattern in cresting should be done as already described.

FIG. 142.

Fig. 130 is a variant on the last design. In this case a little more play of surface is attempted, making a point of carving the side lobes of the leaves into little rounded masses which will reflect points of light. This is shown better in Fig. 142.

In carving foliage like that of the vine, where small, dark holes or eyes occur, enough wood should be left

FIG. 143.

round them to form deep, dark little pits. They are very valuable as points of shadow. In doing this, cut the rim all round with a very slight bevel, as in section, Fig. 143. Whenever leaves run out to a fine edge they should have a small bevel like this, in order to avoid an appearance of weakness which acute edges always present. As a general rule, leave as

No. 1.

No. 2

No. 3.

FIG. 144.

much wood as possible about the edges of leaves, as you want shadow from them—dipping them only where you are sure the variety will be effective. In the execution of bunches of rounded forms like grapes there is no special mechanical expedient for doing them quickly and easily; each must be cut out separately and carved with whatever tools come handiest to their shape and size. It is a good way to begin by cutting triangular holes between the grapes with the point of a

FIG. 145.

small chisel, after which the rough shapes left may gradually be formed into ovals. When the work is very simple in character, and does not require a realistic treatment, the grapes may be done in a more methodical way.

A beautiful example is shown in Fig. 144 of a slip of ivy, where the three stages of drawing, rough-out and finishing are exhibited. No. 1 shows the slip sketched out, No. 2 the rough-out, D D D D showing the stems of the leaves, and E E E the berries. No. 3 shows the work about complete.

What is considered by experts to be one of the most wonderful wood carvings in the world, and which is in the possession of an Italian living in Baltimore, Md., is shown in Fig. 145. He brought it to this country from Italy, where he secured it from a second-hand dealer who did not know of its value.

FIG. 146.

Fig. 146 shows a fine specimen of carving, the original of which was brought from Switzerland by a tourist. This is an excellent piece of work, and is quite natural and forms a suitable finish for a walking cane.

Another good specimen of work which came from the same place is illustrated in Fig. 147. This little bear, a few inches in size, is carved in a way which shows long experience of the subject and great

FIG. 147.

familiarity with the animal's ways. The tooling of the hair is done with the most extraordinary skill, and without the waste of a single touch. Now a word or two more on studies from the life before we leave this subject. We have given examples of diagrams made for this purpose, but much may be done without any drawings further than a preliminary map of the general masses. In the case of such an animal as the horse, which can be seen in every street, it will

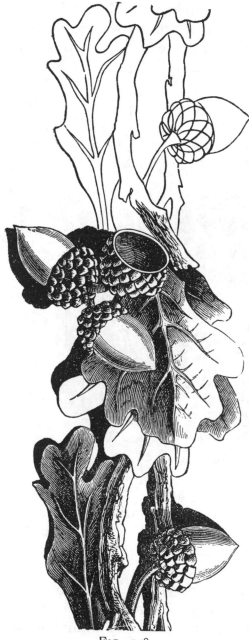

Fig. 148.

be found useful to follow them in their walks, taking mental note of such details as happen to engage your attention, such as the legs and joints, the head or neck; another day confine your attention to eyes, ears, mane, etc., always with reference to the work immediately in hand, as that is the time to get the best results from life study, because the difficulties have presented themselves, and one knows exactly what to look for. Five minutes spent thus after the work has been started (provided the start has been right and involves no mistakes in the general masses) is more valuable than hours of labor in making preliminary drawings.

The use of experi-

mental models in clay or wax has, of course, its advantages, but it will be well to know just how far such an
aid is valuable and at what point its use becomes hurt-

GRAPES AND VINE LEAVES.

Fig. 149.

ful to one's work. It is a common practice in large carving shops for one man to design the figure or animal subjects in clay, while another carves them in stone or wood.

An excellent example for practice is shown in Fig. 148, which exhibits a portion of an oak branch showing complete acorns, leaves, stem and acorn cups. This could be continued for a border, or for the face of a picture frame, and the corner could be made so that the design would be continuous.

FIG. 150.

The full-page design of grapes and vine leaves, Fig. 149, offers a fine chance for expertness with tools. The grapes overlapping each other will require some skill in working them out, and the leaves will also require some delicate handling. This is a beautiful example and should not be attempted until the young workman has every confidence in his own ability to execute it. At any rate, if the workman does not make a satisfactory job of it on the first attempt, he should not be discouraged, but try again and again, and success will surely follow.

The ornament shown in Fig. 150 is composed of mixed work, part of it being turned in the lathe, part of it being carved, and part plain. Moulded work of this kind is often made very beautiful and is frequently employed in architectural work.

CHAPTER VII

INCISED, INTAGLIO, OR SUNK CARVING

This is a style of carving sometimes called deep carving, and by workmen often called "scratch carving"; the proper name, however, is "incised work." A few years ago it was very much employed on furniture, and with very good effect; recently, however, relief work has in a great measure superseded it, and very little of it is now employed.

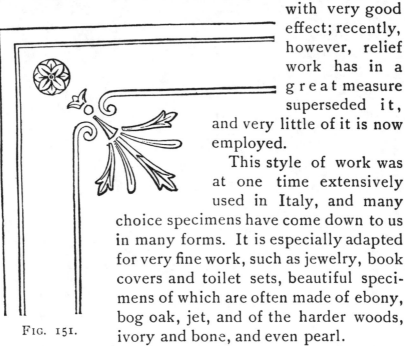

FIG. 151.

This style of work was at one time extensively used in Italy, and many choice specimens have come down to us in many forms. It is especially adapted for very fine work, such as jewelry, book covers and toilet sets, beautiful specimens of which are often made of ebony, bog oak, jet, and of the harder woods, ivory and bone, and even pearl.

This method of carving is very likely of Egyptian origin, as it was used by the monument builders in outlining their figures, which was done by cutting down perpendicularly on the outside and leaving the inside edges just rounded off only, while the inside pattern was not cut away at all. This peculiar method of cutting the groove straight on one side and rounding it off on the other was quite effective and brought out the work in prominent relief and shadow.

This kind of carving is sometimes painted in the incisions and some-times varnished or gilded, which im proves the work very much. White and blue, or vermil-ion, is sometimes employed on t h i s kind of work and when properly done makes a very dainty finish, but black or dark brown is to be preferred, a n d i f gilded in the grooves the effect is quite charming.

It is not intended to say much on the subject of incised carving, but it may not be out of place to give a few illus-trations and sugges-tions on the subject,

SECTION

Fig. 152.

showing what may be done and how to do it so that the young workman may have something to work at by his own fireside to give to his friends if he feels so disposed.

Figs. 151 and 152 are suggestions for a book cover, or for the backs of a blotting case, or any similar work. The material is quite thin, not more than a quarter of an inch thick at the most, and would be even better thinner, and the carving is very shallow.

In making book covers, it is not necessary to make the reverse side elaborate; so in this case the illustration shown in Fig. 151 may be considered the reverse side, which only exhibits a few simple incised lines which are cut with a parting or V tool principally. The other cover, Fig. 152, represents a conventional arrangement of ivy leaves surrounded by a carved moulding, and with a shield in the center for monogram or crest. It may be carved in either boxwood, sycamore, or fine-grained walnut wood. Before commencing the carving it will be necessary that the corners are perfectly square; by this I mean that the angles are right angles, and the object of this is to allow the cover, when finished, to be properly bound. The wood should be about $\frac{1}{4}$ inch in thickness for the front and about $\frac{3}{16}$ inch thick for the reverse side. These carved covers are, in binding, inserted into a sort of panel, and books or blotting pads suitable for carved sides require to be specially made. The best plan is to send the sides when carved to a practical bookbinder to fit on the book when binding. This design, like many others, may easily be enlarged to suit any sized book. The general working and treatment of this pattern will be in every respect similar to others described in this book, and the groundwork may either be punched or left plain at the discretion of the workman. We would, however, call attention to the veining of the leaves. Of course, in natural ivy leaves there are five principal veins with innumerable smaller veins branching out from them, but in carving it is sufficient to show the principal veins *only*, and for variety some of these may be left raised—as in the natural leaf—and the others cut in with a very small veiner. The tendrils shown in the sketch are simply intended to be incised lines only, and not carved in relief like the rest of the design. The moulding round the outside of the cover is sufficiently defined in the illustration and needs no further explanation.

We may now give a brief explanation as to the methods employed and tools and materials required for executing fine small work in art articles or fancy jewelry, such as earrings, bracelets, brooches and similar work. These things may be carved from ebony, bog oak, box-wood, lancewood, or our own iron-wood or hornbeam. These woods may be procured in our large cities from dealers in fret saw and amateur goods generally.

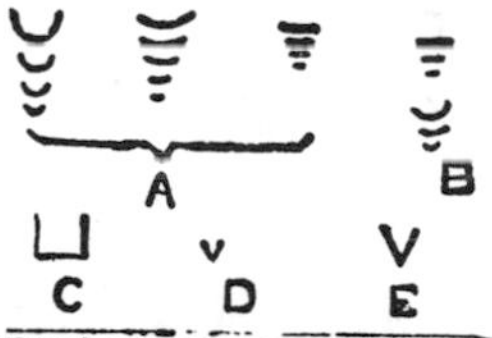

TOOLS FOR EBONY WORK.
ACTUAL SIZE.
A, Straight Tools; B, Bent Tools; C, Maccaroni; D, Veiner; E, Parting Tool.

FIG. 153.

The tools for this kind of work require to be special and may have to be home-made if they cannot be procured from a dealer. It is much better to buy them than to make them, when it is possible to do so. In Fig. 153 I give a sketch of the sizes and sweeps of a few of the tools that will be found most useful, but in addition a very small parting or V tool and the smallest obtainable veiner will be required. Great care must be taken in having the tools sharp, for if not sharp good work is impossible. Another very useful tool is called a "macaroni," and is frequently used for showing raised veins or foliage, etc. The cutting edge is shown at C, Fig. 153, being three sides of a

him. The rough appearance is given to the stem by means of the veiner, parting tool and a small flat tool. The next thing to do is to punch the groundwork,

regulate the fret-cut outlines of the design and put in the necessary veins of the leaves.

The brooch can now be taken up and the glue cleaned off the back. The edges of the leaves require to be chamfered from the back, and the stem

FIG. 155.

rounded off, when we may consider the brooch to be finished, so far as the carving is considered. Ebony should not, except in very few instances, be polished, as it takes an excellent gloss if smartly brushed with a hard

brush which has been slightly moistened with boiled linseed oil. The earrings are carved in exactly the same way, and both can be fret-cut at once by gluing together and marking the outline upon the upper one only. It must be noticed, however, that they be carved in pairs.

The fitting up of the brooch and earrings, Figs. 155 and 156, had better be left to a jeweler, although the amateur can easily do what is necessary if he feels so disposed. The brooch pins and

FIG. 156.

catches can be bought for a few cents (but they should be of gold or silver) from any working jeweler, and with the small veiner the amateur can make the holes in the back of the brooch to admit the pins of the catch. A little powdered shellac should be sprinkled in the holes, and the pins heated in the gas and then placed in position, when, owing to the melting of the shellac, they will be firmly fixed.

Very little trouble will be experienced, we think, by the amateur in making these brooches, etc., from ebony; the only disadvantage is that the wood is rather brittle, but it works firmly under the tool. Often ebony brooches, earrings, crosses, etc., are sold for bog oak or jet; boxwood and other close-grained woods are sometimes dyed black and sold for ebony, bog oak and jet.

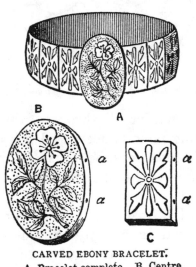

CARVED EBONY BRACELET.
A, Bracelet complete. B, Centre.
C, Side piece.

FIG. 157.

In making bracelets the same rules may, to a large extent, be followed, only in this case it is best to prepare the wood in slips of the requisite width both for the centerpieces and for the small blocks composing the remainder of the bracelet. After cutting these slips, they should be planed slightly hollow on the inside, and the sides also planed so as to fit closely together, and then cut into lengths rather longer than the width of the bracelet.

These blocks can now be glued on a circular piece of pine the size of the inside of the bracelet, and the edges and outside regulated in a turning lathe until the proper thickness and width is obtained; and if the bracelet is to be carved in relief, the depth of the background can also be indicated.

In the case of the centerpieces, it is not of much use to regulate the edges of these, as they will probably be of an oval shape and must be cut with the saw and filed true before being carved. The design can now be carved on the small blocks, which, when finished, will require two small holes bored through each piece, as shown at *a a*, Fig. 157, and these holes can easily be bored in the lathe. In the case of the centerpiece, these holes should be countersunk in order to admit of the knots of the small round elastic on which the blocks are threaded and which serve to keep the bracelet together. To ensure uniformity, the holes should

Section along A A.

EXAMPLE OF INCISED WORK.

FIG. 158.

all be bored at equal distances. After this has been done the bracelet may be considered complete.

The ornamentation may consist either of a relieved design, or the centerpiece only may be in relief, and the remainder of the pattern may be incised, as in Fig. 157. It is a mistake to make these bracelets too heavy, but the size must, of course, be left to the individual fancy of the amateur, as the design here given is only offered as a suggestion.

Other articles of personal ornament may be carved in ebony, such as pins for the hair, buttons, etc., but in every case it is better to leave the wood dull and not brightly polished.

We will now give a few directions for the incised work which will be of greater service to all amateur wood carvers than the previous examples. This style of decoration consists in the design being simply incised, or in first incising the lines round the object and then carving the surface within to correspond with the various parts of the design. The ground is thus left standing and the object sunk below the level of the ground, although the surface of the ornament itself is carved, an example of which is seen in Fig. 158, the surface of the design being indicated by the section along the line A A.

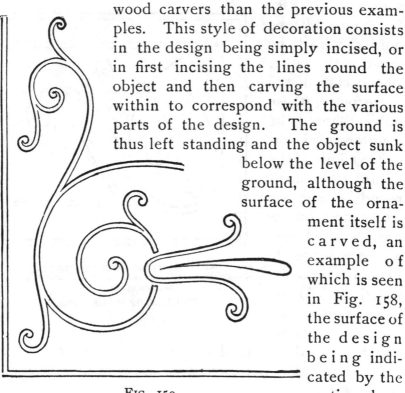

Fig. 159.

Incised work is suitable for a variety of articles used in indoor decoration, and is often applied most effectively to the ornamentation of piano fronts, furniture of every description, brackets and picture frames. The work is easy to do, needing only a thorough command of the tools, combined with delicacy of touch and a good eye for graceful lines, the manual labor required being absolutely nil, and nearly any design is applicable.

Incised work may also be done in any w o o d, the incised portion being left of the natural color of the wood, or stained. The first process is to stain and polish the wood; the design is then marked on the surface and the incised portion cut out, the work being again polished to obliterate a n y a c c i d e n t a l scratches, and the exposed portions of the design are gilded in oil; when the surface of the wood is black, any mistake or accidental slip of the tool is easily rectified by

FIG. 160.

filling up the cut with glue and sawdust. There are several methods adopted for transferring the design to the wood. We will describe two and allow our readers to take their choice. One plan is to trace the design on ordinary tracing paper and then to paste the tracing thus obtained on to a piece of cardboard, leaving here and there a narrow strip of the cardboard to support and keep the pattern together, as is done in stencil plates. The patterns can be cut out very accurately with the aid of the carving tools, which will be found better suited to this purpose than a penknife. The cardboard is then placed on the wood and the pattern either shown by being dusted on with a "pounce" composed of whiting enclosed in a piece of linen, or marked off with a needle point.

Fig. 161.

Another plan, which, if not so effective, certainly entails far less work, is to trace the design on tracing paper and then place the tracing paper on the wood and again go over the design with a sharp point of ivory, which leaves a slight indentation on the surface of the polish. Designs consisting simply of lines without broader ornament are incised in either of the methods shown in Fig. 159, being cut with a veiner or a parting or V tool. When, however, the design is of a more complicated nature, consisting of lines and floral or other ornamentation, and it is desired to curve the surface of the design, a different system of working must be pursued. The lines should first be cut with a parting tool, and then set in and regulated with carving tools of the proper shape, after which the ornament should be treated in the same way as in the case of a panel. We have in Figs. 159 and 160 given examples of both kinds of incised ornament.

When there are straight lines in a design, the "scratch" tool will prove of great service, but care must be taken in using it not to scratch the surface of the polish.

The round holes so often seen in incised work are made by first roughly cutting with a quick tool and then regulating with "roly-polies" of various sizes. This instrument is used

Fig. 162.

by being rapidly twirled round between the hands, and is most serviceable.

As to the actual method to be adopted in working these incised patterns, some carvers adopt one plan and some another; one man, for instance, will go roughly over the whole design and then go carefully over it again to finish off, whilst another will finish completely piece by piece of the design. In working scroll lines, it is advisable to regulate the outlines with carving tools, as neither the parting tool nor veiner will cut in every direction of the grain so clean as to avoid occasionally tearing the wood. Where the V shape is preferred, all the intricate portions of the design can be cut and finished with the tools alone. In incised work, it is customary to use carving tools of the shape known as "spade" tools, probably owing to the shape being somewhat similar to that useful implement.

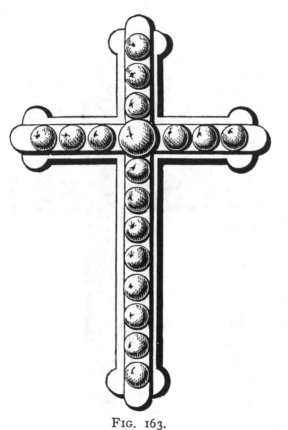

FIG. 163.

We would strongly advise any of our readers who may feel inclined to try the incised work, to avoid doing it by gas or artificial light, as it is very trying to the eyes, and the same remark holds good with reference to ebony carving. As to the best kind of designs for incising, we think it advisable to select those composed chiefly of scroll or flowing lines. All incised work loses effect, unless great care be taken to have the lines correct, as owing to the contrast between the black and the gold the smallest defect in regularity is at once apparent

The best woods are those having a firm, close grain, such as sycamore, holly or pear tree, all of which, in addition to being easily carved, also have the advantage of taking stain readily; coarse and cross-grained woods are to be avoided, as being unfit for this class of work.

CHAPTER VIII

MISCELLANEOUS ITEMS

In this, the closing chapter, we have deemed it proper to give a few examples of finished work of various kinds in order to provide designs for work the young carver may think proper to undertake, and which, we feel, he can execute now, after having followed the instructions and directions given in the previous chapters.

FIG. 164.

The first designs presented are for crosses, suitable for church service; they may be made large or small to suit conditions, or they may be made for covers of prayer or hymn books, or for a dozen other purposes. The one shown in Fig. 161 is quite a plain one and will not prove a severe tax on the skill of the workman. Fig. 162 is somewhat more elaborate, but simple in design withal and not difficult to execute.

FIG. 165.

The design shown in Fig. 163 is a very pretty one, and if the arms of the cross are made of ebony, bog oak or teak, and the bottom of ivory or pearl, it will make a very showy and effective piece of work, but it would not be in the best of taste.

Another simple design is shown in Fig. 164. The coils around it may be formed by silver or gold wire. In either case the complete work would be chaste and quite pretty.

FIG. 166.

The full-page design shown in Fig. 165 is a fine piece of work and would do admirably for the cover of a large prayer-book or Bible, and would not tax the carver to any great extent. The clover leaves are not difficult to follow, and the lapping over would be found an easy matter after what has gone before.

Another design for a book cover is shown in Fig. 166, and one which is sure to be appreciated. I. H. S. is always in order on covers of books intended for church service, and the design shown is really an

FIG. 167

excellent one for the purpose, and will, we are sure, be made use of by many readers of this when preparing Christmas presents.

INTERIOR VIEW OF CARVED WOODEN DOUBLE OUTER DOORS.
FIG. 168.

These examples of crosses are quite sufficient for the present, and if our readers desire other designs

they may be found among illustrations shown in our
current literature, and we would advise the young
carver to be always on the "lookout" for designs of

JEWEL OR TRINKET BOX, WITH CARVED PANEL.

FIG. 169.

all kinds that are likely to become useful for work he
may sometime have to undertake. It is a good way
to have a scrapbook kept purposely for designs of

FIG. 170.

carved work, and to paste in it anything the carver
may think will some day be of use to him.

The full-page designs of "Gothic" ornamentation

FIG. 171.

show almost every phase of Gothic carved work, with
the exception of figure carving, but this has been well
set forth in the chapter devoted to that style of carving. The six examples shown in Fig. 167 are taken

from actual work, and were drawn from "The Art Amateur." These will supply the carver with almost every motive he may ever require in this peculiar style.

Another full-page design, for a pair of doors, is shown in Fig. 168. This is in the Cincinnati style of carving, a school introduced some years ago by Benn Pitman, and which was for a time quite popular. It will be seen that the architraves or casings, head mouldings, plinth blocks and base are carved, as well as the doors. Some of the work done by the pupils of Benn Pitman was exceedingly good, but the style, from some cause or other, did not seem to

A little Carved Coffee Table.

FIG. 172.

"catch on" firm enough to stay, though some of this work is still employed. The trouble with this style of work seems to be a lack of robustness and vigor. Apart from this lack, the style possesses many redeeming qualities and much refinement, and it is a pity it is not made more use of than at present.

The design shown in Fig. 169 is intended for a small box that may be used for gloves, handkerchiefs, jewelry or trinkets of any kind. The top figure shows the box with half the carved front; the lower design shows the carving on the lid or cover. It will be seen that there are four claws supporting the box. These may be dispensed with if desired.

FIG. 173.

The two examples shown in Fig. 170 exhibit perforated carved work, and are good examples of German carving. They may be used for hat racks or for key boards, and may be made larger or smaller to suit the purpose for which they are intended. There is some fine work on the lower design. In Fig. 171 we show

a small clock case finished with simple carvings. This piece of work is well within the reach of every one who has learned to use carvers' tools.

The little coffee table shown in Fig. 172 is one that may be made at home and carved by any carpenter. The design is quite simple.

In Fig. 173 we show a design for a drawer front; this is rather a handsome piece of work.

The design shown in Fig. 174 is for a carved table leg and is a very fine piece of work. We are indebted to the "Woodworker" for this design and some others we have made use of, and for which we offer our thanks.

The carved panel shown in Fig. 175

FIG. 174.

FIG. 175.

offers suggestions to the carver which, no doubt, he
will make use of as opportunity occurs.

The two designs for borders shown in Fig. 176 may

FIG. 176.

be employed in many situations, and require little or
no explanation, as they speak for themselves.

It is quite "the thing" now to have drawer fronts

FIG. 177.

carved, and the two illustrations shown in Fig. 177
have been designed for that purpose. Both are admirably adapted to the purpose and are so designed that

Fig. 178.

but a fair exercise of skill will be required in their execution. We commend these to our readers as being excellent examples for the purpose designed.

The corner cupboard shown in Fig. 178 exhibits some elaborate carvings, and while it appears to be

FIG. 179.

rather overdone, it offers an opportunity for exercise that few pieces of furniture can afford. The plain cupboard in itself is a very simple affair, but the carver's chisel has added much to its value and appearance.

One of the first ambitions of a young carver is to be able to carve a photo frame, and to satisfy this laudable ambition we present a few designs for this purpose. The one shown in Fig. 179 is a very simple affair, but

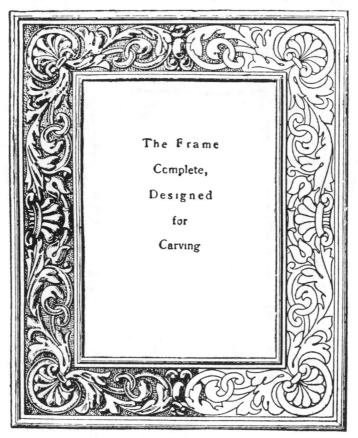

The Frame
Complete,
Designed
for
Carving

FIG. 180.

is quite effective when the work is neatly done.   The frame shown in Fig. 180 is a much more pretentious one and requires a lot of labor to make it look well, but it is so arranged that it can be made large enough to take in pictures of any reasonable size.   It would

answer very nicely for a mirror frame or for a fine
steel engraving or etching.   It is a very nice piece of
work and requires some fine handling to make it

FIG. 181.

effective.   The wheat ears in this example, shown in
Fig. 181, and the one following are worth carefully
attending to, as they are constantly introduced into
woodwork; and being solid, and forming good masses

Fig. 182.

of light and shade, are very suitable for relief to foliage. First chisel out the shape of the whole ear, without considering each separate grain; round it well and see that the relief is good; then draw on the wood with a soft pencil the outline of the grains, or, if uncertain, trace them on soft paper and paste it on the surface of the ear (the carver, of course, does not use the design to work upon, but traces from it, so that he can always

FIG. 183.

refer to his model); then, when dry, chisel out each grain carefully, giving it a good rounded surface with a well-defined form, and you will be surprised with the results.

The same remarks will answer for the working of the design shown in Fig. 182.

The two pediments shown in Fig. 183 may be classed as "architectural" carving, and are given here merely to show what an immense field there is lying open for the young man who is determined to follow this art as a business. Indeed, there is no limit to this branch of decorative art, as there is nothing made of wood or stone where the carver's chisel may not be employed to enhance the value and the beauty of the work.

In conclusion, we add two examples of carved chair backs that are simple in design and which may be employed in decorating chairs now in use (see Fig. 184).

In closing this volume, I think it but fair to say that I have drawn largely from the best authorities on

FIGS. 184 AND 185.

the subject, to which I have added the results of my own experience, which is somewhat extended, and I think, after looking over the book and carefully noting both text and illustrations, my efforts to make a useful and instructive book on the "Art of Wood Carving" have not been altogether in vain, and I sincerely hope my readers will derive as much benefit from it as will enable them to not only carve in wood, but also give them a fair knowledge of the art of designing subjects suitable to any work in carving they may undertake.

INDEX